Furrows and Hedgerows

MY REFLECTIONS OF FARM, FOOD AND FAMILY

Rosemary Perry

Editor: Jane F. Perry Becker
Consultant: Marilyn A. Perry Galbreath
Copy Editing by Sheila Mauck
Cover and Book Design by Cathy Swick

Publisher
Thyme with Rosemary Books
Rosemary Perry
2548 Robinwood Drive
Lafayette, Indiana 47909

First Printing

Published by Thyme with Rosemary Books, Rosemary Perry
2548 Robinwood Drive, Lafayette, Indiana 47909

Library of Congress Catalogue Card Number 00-190448

Perry, Rosemary
Furrows and Hedgerows: My Reflections of Farm, Food and Family
Index Included

ISBN 0-9679531-0-3

First Printing

Printed by
Starr*Toof
670 South Cooper Street
Memphis, TN 38104

DEDICATED TO THE PERRYS

Zephir Perry .... Great Grandfather 1857

Pauline Balthazar Perry .... Great Grandmother 1864

Leujay J. Perry .... Grandfather 1887

Bertha E. Lebold Perry .... Grandmother 1891

Albert Brucker .... Grandfather 1885

Lydia Wade Brucker .... Grandmother 1887

Lawrence J. Perry, Sr. .... Father 1917

Mary Jane Brucker Perry .... Mother 1924

Lawrence J. Perry, Jr. .... Brother 1943

James A. Perry .... Brother 1944

Rosemary Perry .... Self 1946

Albert L. Perry .... Brother 1947

Michael L. Perry .... Brother 1949

Marilyn A. Perry Galbreath .... Sister 1952

Kathleen M. Perry Weidner .... Sister 1957

Jane F. Perry Becker .... Sister 1964

Michael H. Yoder .... Son 1970

Lesly L. Yoder Norris .... Daughter 1976

Shelby L. Yoder .... Granddaughter 1993

Bailey R. Norris .... Granddaughter 1996

Kaitlyn M. Norris .... Granddaughter 1998

Great Grandfather Zephir Perry originally acquired the ninety-two acres that was passed down and that my parents currently call home.

ACKNOWLEDGMENTS

My family and friends have my fondest appreciation for helping make this book a reality. Without my family, the dream of writing this book would not have been possible. My memories are indelible of a disappearing way of life given to me by my parents on their family farm in northwest Indiana. I give my deepest thank you to my parents and to my four brothers and three sisters who have all contributed to the making of this book.

To Mike and Lesly, my two children, and Shelby, Bailey and Kaitlyn, my three beautiful granddaughters, I give my deepest appreciation for their loving support. It is for them and their children to come that I have written this book to preserve our family memories.

Two of my loving sisters, Jane F. Perry Becker and Marilyn A. Perry Galbreath, have given tirelessly of their talents with unmentioned hours of editing each page and consulting. We are a team of sisters who give and take willingly and immeasurably of each other.

Margie Stein and Vicki Clark are special friends who have encouraged and supported me since the first day they knew I wanted to write *Furrows and Hedgerows.* I am fortunate to have these two friends and all other friends who have tirelessly listened and helped.

Thank you to all the readers of my newspaper column, Thyme with Rosemary, for their overwhelming generosity and enthusiasm. They have cheered me on from week to week.

TABLE OF CONTENTS

REMEMBRANCES 7

HERB SEASONINGS 9

FINGER FOODS 13

BREAD 25

BREAKFAST BREADS 41

MUFFINS 59

SOUPS 73

SALADS 85

MEAT & POTATOES 105

VEGETABLES 125

CAKE & ICE CREAM 133

CHEESECAKES 149

PIES 159

COOKIES & DESSERTS 175

CANDY 191

JAM, JELLY, ETC. 199

REFRESHERS 213

Remembrances

One of my fondest childhood memories finds me in a hedgerow. A hedgerow seems an odd place for a memory, but these closely planted trees were a haven in which to find peace and contentment. In earlier years farm fields were divided by growing hedgerows. Rows of Osage Orange trees were planted close together to form a fence. The fence of thorny limbs and branches contained farm animals, provided windbreaks for animals and buildings and helped prevent soil erosion. Hedgerows were trimmed by hand with well-sharpened corn knives twice each summer to keep them at a desired height. Farmers would trim hedge around buildings and along the roadside, and leave hedge-dividing fields to grow tall.

More hedges were easy to start by planting the hedge apples produced by the trees. Straight limbs were difficult to find, but the least crooked limbs were used for fence posts. The rock-hard wood from the Osage trees was a challenge to work with. Hedge posts last a lifetime; never rotting. Small pieces of wire were used to fasten barbed wire or woven wire to the posts. Staples or nails could not be used because of the rock-hard wood. Hedge fence posts put in before 1943 still stand along a ditch bank on our farm.

Hedgerows served many purposes in earlier eras. Large hedgerows provided sanctuaries for birds, rabbits, fox, deer and many other wild animals. The trees grew large, using acreage needed for crops, and drank moisture from the earth. Today hedgerows are all but gone.

Furrows are made when plowing a field. Plowing turns the earth over, preparing the soil for planting in the spring. Springtime plowing was the start of each growing season. We liked the smell of the freshly turned earth. As Dad plowed, the turning of the soil formed a furrow. A furrow looks like a groove, long and straight. A favorite pastime of Dad's young children was to run barefoot behind the plow in the freshly formed furrow. The soil was still cool and damp on our bare feet.

Dad's definition of a good farmer was by how straight he plowed a furrow. Dad plowed his furrows by watching the posts at the other end of the field; he had the straightest furrows of any farmer. He and Mom raised us children with the same straightforward concept. There was only one way of doing anything. It was the right way, with the highest standards. Dad said a good farmer father taught his children to scratch out a chicken lot of their own.

Furrows and hedgerows are symbolic of the Perry family. Furrows are beginnings, fresh and new. Hedgerows endure for a lifetime, strong, protective and well remembered.

I am a native Hoosier born in the post-World War II years. My family has called Indiana home for four generations, with another two generations following me. I am the third of eight children. Mom and Dad Perry reared my four brothers and three sisters on a farm in northern Indiana. The first ninety-two acres of land was purchased by my great grandfather, Zephir Pare' (Perry). My cooking skills were honed at home first due to the necessity to help my mother and then because I enjoyed it.

The center of our home was the kitchen. Mom was usually in the kitchen when we bounded off the yellow school bus, and when Dad came in from the fields or barn. Visitors instinctively gathered around the kitchen table.

Absolutely no eating of a meal was started before grace was said. Meals at our dinner table were surrounded with Dad at the head of the table, Mom at his immediate left, and came to full circle with all the Perry children. The youngest baby sat in a wood high chair at the corner of the table between our parents. The oldest boy sat at the opposite end of Dad.

When I was eleven years old Mom delivered my sister Kathy, and then Mom had Jane when I was eighteen. Being the oldest daughter, I took responsibility preparing all the meals for our family and caring for my younger siblings while she was in the hospital. This included a complete Christmas dinner prepared for all, together with my grandparents, Leujay and Bertha Perry.

Fieldwork, tending to farm animals and gathering eggs were considered work for Dad and the boys. Gardening, housework and caring for the children were considered work for Mom and the girls. Regardless, we helped one another. During spring planting or harvest, Mom drove a tractor or truck to help Dad, and took many meals to the field. When fresh fruit or vegetables were ready to can, Dad and the boys pitted cherries, stemmed strawberries and snapped beans. Our young years provided my brothers, sisters and me with responsibility, caring and the organizational skills for adult life. All the special times spent working, playing and praying together has attained a special family togetherness that will last forever. The simplicity of our farm life has led us to achieve a satisfying, rewarding life.

Many of this book's treasured recipes come from my Hoosier heritage along with favorites gathered from more recent years. A mere glimpse of the past is offered in *Furrows and Hedgerows* to preserve memories not only for my parents and siblings, but also for my children and their children's families.

Rosemary

Over the years I have developed my own herb seasoning mixes to use on meats and vegetables and in soups. Our garden at home usually had parsley, chives and sage. Adult life found me growing garlic, thyme, oregano, tarragon and many more herbs for their flavorful additions to my everyday cooking. I enjoy walking through my garden and brushing past basil, rosemary and lemon verbena to release their heady scents. The end of a rain shower brings a delightful blend of smells from my garden. Bring bouquets of herbs into your home for fresh kitchen table arrangements, or hang to dry. Herbs give unspeakable comforts of contentment and peacefulness to a being.

In early summer the garden is lush and fragrant with tender new growth, and it is time to start harvesting the herbs. From June through the first of September I harvest the top third of each branch. The herbs will keep trim and neat as the plants spread sideways. Harvesting monthly will prevent the plants from flowering and forming seed heads. Of course, some herbs such as oregano, sage and lemon verbena have lovely flowers. I have plenty of these herbs to harvest and a few to let flower. The flowering herbs add beauty and fragrance to bouquets. A day or a few hours before harvesting, I use a fine hose to spray the herbs. On the early morning of the harvest, I wait until the leaves are dry, and then harvest the herbs.

Gathering and drying herbs each growing season provides me with the freshest and thus most flavorful herbs to make my seasoning mixes. Fresh herbs add wonderful flavors to any meat, poultry, seafood, pasta or vegetable dish. Herbs may be found at your local farmer's market, at herb farms and at your supermarket. Only when fresh herbs are not readily available use dried. Drying your own will assure you of the finest quality. Dried herbs should be discarded after one year because of loss of flavor.

PHOTO ~ *Rosemary Perry,* myself

Rosemary's Roast Beef Seasoning

. . . . . .

3 tablespoons dried parsley
2 tablespoons dried rosemary
2 tablespoons dried chives
1 tablespoon dried summer savory
1 tablespoon dried minced garlic
1 tablespoon dried thyme

Chop herbs. Mix well and store in a glass jar.
Makes about 1/2 cup.

. . . . . .

Or (for a larger amount):
2 cups dried parsley
1 1/4 cups dried rosemary
1 1/4 cup dried chives
1/2 cup plus 1 tablespoon dried summer savory
1/2 cup plus 1 tablespoon dried minced garlic
1/2 cup plus 1 tablespoon dried thyme

Chop herbs. Mix well and store in a glass jar.
Use 2 to 3 tablespoons per 3- to 5-pound roast, or to taste.
Makes about 1 1/2 quarts.

Rosemary's Soup Seasoning Mix

· · · · · ·

This mix is good sprinkled on steaks while grilling.

1 cup dried parsley
1 cup dried thyme
1 cup dried marjoram
1/2 cup dried summer savory
1/4 cup dried basil
1/8 cup dried rosemary
2 to 3 bay leaves, crushed

Chop herbs. Mix well and store in a glass jar.
Use 1 to 2 tablespoons per quart of soup, or to taste.
Makes 3 1/2 to 4 cups.

Rosemary's Pork Seasoning

· · · · · ·

1 teaspoon dried thyme
1/2 teaspoon dried rosemary
4 tablespoons dried parsley
1 teaspoon dried minced garlic

Chop herbs. Mix well and store in a glass jar.
Use 2 to 3 tablespoons per 3- to 5-pound roast, or to taste.
Makes 5 tablespoons.

Rosemary's Fish Seasoning Mix

. . . . . .

5 tablespoons dried dill
5 tablespoons dried basil
5 tablespoons dried fennel leaves
5 tablespoons dried parsley

Chop herbs. Mix well and store in a glass jar.
Sprinkle onto fish or seafood before baking or grilling.
Makes 1 1/4 cups.

Cajun Seasoned Salt

. . . . . .

Marilyn enjoys cooking Cajun. She gave me this lively blend of spices, essential to most Cajun dishes. She suggests seasoning catfish fillets or pork chops liberally with this spice mix before broiling.

1/4 cup salt
2 tablespoons cayenne pepper
2 tablespoons paprika
1 1/2 tablespoons onion powder
1 tablespoon freshly ground black pepper
1 tablespoon freshly ground white pepper
1 tablespoon garlic powder
2 teaspoons dried basil
1 teaspoon chili powder
1/4 teaspoon dried thyme
1/4 teaspoon ground mustard
1/8 teaspoon ground cloves

Combine all ingredients in a small jar.
Spice mix can be stored in a tightly covered glass jar in a cool, dry place out of direct light
    for up to 4 months.
Makes about 3/4 cup.

Finger Foods

When we still had the old two-story barn on the farm, the first floor had stalls for milking the cows, an area for the cows to stay after milking and several grain bins. The partitioned wood bins in the old barn were of different sizes, some with slatted walls for corn still on the cobs, some with no slats for the oats and wheat. Dad sold most of his grain while harvesting in the fall of the year. Corn and oats were stored in the wood bins to be fed to the farm cattle and chickens.

We young'uns liked to play in the corn and in the bins of grain. Dad always told us to stay out of the oats, but sometimes we didn't listen well. The chaff from the wheat and oats left on our clothes would tattle on us, not to mention how itchy the chaff was to our bodies. When the bins were empty, they made great places for us to take our toys to play. The door leading from the outside of the barn to the two milking stalls was divided with a lower half and an upper half. The upper half could be left open, without the cows leaving the barn.

Thank goodness the house was painted white with blue aluminum awnings over the windows. Dad painted his buildings bright orange with white trim instead of the customary red barn trimmed with white. Prior to Dad's orange buildings, Mom's father, Albert Brucker, painted his farm buildings the same color of orange. The orange paint was called Big Four Yellow. The Big Four railroad painted all of their cabooses with Big Four Yellow. Giving directions to our home, we would direct them to the orange buildings.

PHOTO ~ *Bertha and Leujay Perry,* my grandparents

Tomato Basil Sandwiches

. . . . . .

Serve for a tea party.

Butter:
1/2 cup unsalted butter, cut up
1 teaspoon tomato puree
1/4 teaspoon sugar
1/4 teaspoon salt
1/4 teaspoon fresh lemon juice
1/4 cup lightly packed fresh basil, chopped, or 1 tablespoon dried basil

In a food processor, combine butter, tomato puree, sugar, salt and lemon juice. Process until blended. Add basil leaves. Pulse until mixed. Set aside at room temperature.

Filling:
1 pound fresh tomatoes

Plunge tomatoes into boiling water 20 to 30 seconds. Cool in cold water. Drain.
Peel, core and seed tomatoes. Chop tomatoes very fine. Stir gently in a strainer to drain.

Sandwiches:
Slices of white and wheat bread
Salt and pepper to taste

Just before serving, spread 1 side of each slice of white and whole wheat breads with basil butter.
Spread tomato filling on white bread. Season with salt and pepper. Top with wheat bread, buttered
  side down. Cut each sandwich in fourths, diagonally.
Makes 16 to 20 sandwiches.

Shrimp Cheese Ball

. . . . . .

Winter holidays are perfect for serving this special cheese ball.

2 3-ounce packages cream cheese, softened
1 teaspoon prepared mustard
1 teaspoon onion, grated
1 teaspoon fresh lemon juice
Few grains cayenne pepper
Dash salt
1 4 1/2-ounce can shrimp, drained and broken into pieces
2/3 cup salted, mixed nuts, chopped

Beat cream cheese and blend with mustard, onion, lemon juice, pepper and salt. Stir shrimp pieces into mixture and chill well. Form into small 1/2-inch balls and roll each into chopped nuts.
Makes 3 dozen.

Sun-dried Tomato and Pesto Torte

. . . . .

This torte is always a hit! Not only for its perfect combination of sun-dried tomatoes, basil pesto and goat cheese, but also for its unusual attractiveness.

Pesto:
2 cups fresh basil leaves
1/2 cup parsley leaves
1/2 cup olive oil
3 tablespoons walnuts
2 garlic cloves, peeled
1/4 cup grated Parmesan cheese
2 tablespoons butter, softened
Salt to taste

Puree the basil, parsley, olive oil, nuts and garlic in a food processor or blender.
Mix in the cheese and butter by hand. Season to taste.

Torte:
1 8-ounce package cream cheese, softened
12 ounces goat cheese
1/2 pound (2 sticks) butter, softened
1 cup basil pesto (see recipe, above)
1 cup sun-dried tomatoes, drained and minced
Assorted crackers

Place the cheeses and butter in a bowl and beat together until they are well blended and fluffy.
Line an 8-inch cake pan with dampened cheesecloth, leaving enough extra cheesecloth to fold
   over the top.
Layer one-third of the cheese mixture in the bottom and spread half the pesto over it. Repeat. Spread
   the remaining cheese on top and cover with the minced tomatoes. Place a piece of plastic wrap over
   the top and fold the cheesecloth over it. Set the torte in the refrigerator for at least an hour to
   firm up. When ready to serve, fold the cheesecloth back, turn the torte onto a plate and remove
   the cheesecloth. Invert the torte onto a serving plate and remove the plastic wrap.
Serve with assorted crackers.
Serves 30 to 40. Freezes well.

Marinated Mushrooms

. . . . .

A company pleaser.

2 pounds fresh mushrooms, well cleaned
1 tablespoon butter
1 tablespoon parsley, chopped
1 lemon, halved
1 cup dry red wine
1/4 cup wine vinegar
1/2 cup olive oil
1 teaspoon tarragon
1/4 teaspoon ground cloves
1 shallot, chopped
Salt and pepper

Place mushrooms, butter and parsley in saucepan. Squeeze juice from lemon halves, add to saucepan
and season well. Pour in wine, vinegar and olive oil. Mix well.

Add remaining ingredients, season and cook, covered, 8 to 10 minutes over high heat. Stir once or
twice during cooking. Cool mushrooms before serving.

Serves 10 to 12.

Cocktail Shrimp

. . . . . .

Serve this wonderful appetizer for special occasions with special friends and/or family. They will thank you!

3 pounds jumbo shrimp
1/4 cup dry sherry
6 cups water
3/4 cup olive oil
2/3 cup white wine vinegar
1 tablespoon fresh tarragon, minced, or 3/4 teaspoon dried tarragon
1 1/2 teaspoons sugar
1 1/2 teaspoons salt
3/4 teaspoon crushed red pepper

Shell and devein shrimp but leave tail part of shell on.
In a 4-quart saucepan over high heat, heat sherry and 6 cups water to boiling. Add shrimp and heat
    to boiling, stirring often. Reduce heat to low; simmer 1 minute or until shrimp are pink on
    outside and opaque inside. Drain.
In a large bowl, stir together olive oil, white wine vinegar, tarragon, sugar, salt and crushed red
    pepper. Add shrimp and toss to coat with marinade. Cover and marinate shrimp in refrigerator
    at least 6 hours or overnight, tossing occasionally.
Drain before serving.
Serves 6 to 8.

Smoked Salmon-Stuffed Cherry Tomatoes

. . . . . .

Simply delicious!

1 pint cherry tomatoes
1 8-ounce package cream cheese, softened
1/4 pound smoked salmon, sliced
4 teaspoons fresh dill, minced, or 3/4 teaspoon dried dill weed
1 teaspoon fresh lemon juice

(continued on next page)

Cut each cherry tomato crosswise in half. Remove seeds and pulp from cherry tomatoes to form cups; discard seeds and pulp. Place cherry-tomato cups, cut-side down, on paper towels to drain.

In a food processor with a knife blade attached, blend cream cheese, smoked salmon, dill and lemon juice until mixture is smooth.

Spoon smoked salmon mixture into a small decorating bag with a large star tube. Pipe salmon mixture into cherry-tomato cups. Arrange cherry tomatoes on a platter. Cover loosely with plastic wrap and refrigerate until ready to serve.

Makes about 50.

Shrimp-Stuffed Eggs

. . . . .

6 large eggs
1 4-ounce can small shrimp, rinsed and drained
1 teaspoon parsley, chopped
2 tablespoons butter, softened
3 tablespoons mayonnaise
1/4 teaspoon paprika
Few drops fresh lemon juice
Few drops Worcestershire sauce
Salt and pepper
Extra parsley, chopped

Cook eggs 10 minutes in gently boiling water. When cooked, drain and cool under running water for at least 3 to 5 minutes. Peel cooled eggs and cut in half, lengthwise.

Carefully remove yolks and place in a sieve set over a bowl. Force through with a spoon or pestle. Scrape bottom of sieve to gather all the yolks. Set aside in bowl.

Pat shrimp dry with paper towel. Place in food processor along with parsley and puree.

Transfer shrimp and parsley to bowl containing sieved yolks. Add butter and mix well. Stir in mayonnaise until well incorporated. Season with paprika, lemon juice, Worcestershire sauce, salt and pepper. Mix well. Arrange the egg-white halves on a plate. Spoon shrimp filling into a pastry bag fitted with a large star tube. Force filling into egg-white halves. Sprinkle with chopped parsley.

Serves 6 to 8.

Fresh Tomato Chili Dip

. . . . . .

Great for back-yard barbecues and picnics or a snack.

4 large tomatoes, chopped
8 green onions, chopped
8 to 10 fresh chilies or 2 4-ounce cans chilies, chopped
1 4 1/4-ounce can ripe olives, chopped and drained
6 tablespoons red wine vinegar
1 tablespoon olive oil
2 to 3 garlic cloves, pressed through garlic press
1 fresh jalapeño pepper, seeded and chopped
Tortilla chips

Place tomatoes and onions into a large bowl. Stir in the next five ingredients. Add jalapeño pepper.
Cover and refrigerate overnight. Serve with tortilla chips.
Makes 2 to 3 cups.

Tomato Cheese Spread

. . . . . .

1/3 cup oil-packed dried tomatoes, drained
2 tablespoons of the oil from dried tomatoes
1 8-ounce package cream cheese
1/4 cup butter, softened
1/2 cup grated Parmesan cheese
1 tablespoon fresh basil, chopped, or 1 teaspoon dried basil
Dash salt
Assorted crackers and/or bagels

Place dried tomatoes in a food processor and pulse several times until tomatoes are in tiny pieces.
Remove. Combine oil, cheese, butter, Parmesan cheese and fresh basil and blend until smooth.
   Stir in tomato pieces. Cover and chill.
Serve with crackers or bagels.
Makes 2 cups.

Shrimp Spread

. . . . . .

1 8-ounce package cream cheese, softened
1/2 cup sour cream
1/4 cup mayonnaise
1 cup seafood cocktail sauce
2 cups light mozzarella cheese, shredded
2 4 1/2-ounce cans shrimp, rinsed and drained
3 green onions, chopped
3/4 cup tomato, finely chopped
Assorted crackers or nacho chips

In a small mixing bowl, beat cream cheese, sour cream and mayonnaise until smooth. Spread on a
    12-inch round serving platter. Cover with seafood sauce. Sprinkle with cheese, shrimp, onions and
    tomato. Cover and chill.
Serve with crackers or nacho chips.
Makes 5 cups.

Salmon Party Spread

. . . . . .

This spread is devoured in minutes.

1 8-ounce package cream cheese, at room temperature
1 7 1/2-ounce can pink salmon, drained, flaked and cartilage removed
3 tablespoons fresh parsley, chopped
2 tablespoons green bell pepper, finely chopped
2 tablespoons sweet red pepper, finely chopped
2 teaspoons onion, grated
1 teaspoon fresh lemon juice
1 teaspoon prepared horseradish
1/2 teaspoon liquid smoke, optional
Pecans or additional parsley, finely chopped
Assorted crackers

Combine the first nine ingredients in a bowl and stir until well blended. Cover and chill 2 to 24 hours.
Transfer to a serving bowl and sprinkle with pecans or parsley. Serve with crackers.
Makes 2 cups.

Black Bean Dip

. . . . .

4 garlic cloves, peeled
Water
1 15- to 19-ounce can black beans, rinsed and drained
2 tablespoons tomato paste
2 tablespoons olive oil
4 1/2 teaspoons fresh lime juice
1/2 teaspoon cumin, ground
1/2 teaspoon coriander, ground
1/4 teaspoon salt
1/8 teaspoon red cayenne pepper, ground
1 tablespoon water

In a 1-quart saucepan, place garlic and enough water to cover. Heat to boiling over high heat. Reduce heat to low; cover and simmer 3 minutes to blanch garlic; drain.
In a food processor with a knife blade attached, blend garlic with remaining ingredients until smooth. Spoon dip into a bowl; cover and refrigerate up to 2 days.
Makes about 2 cups.

Crab Dip

. . . . .

Try this wonderful old-fashioned dip with chilled Chardonnay.

3/4 cup mayonnaise
3 tablespoons prepared horseradish
3 tablespoons onion, finely chopped
1 tablespoon Worcestershire sauce
12 ounces crabmeat
Hot pepper sauce (such as Tabasco)
Salt and pepper to taste
Assorted Belgian endive spears, celery sticks, carrot sticks and bell pepper strips
Assorted crackers and breadsticks

Mix first 4 ingredients in a medium bowl. Mix in crab. Season to taste with hot pepper sauce, salt and pepper. Cover and chill. Serve with assorted vegetables, crackers and breadsticks.
Makes 1 1/2 to 2 cups.

Hill Country Salsa

. . . . . .

This salsa recipe comes from my sister, Marilyn.

1 15-ounce can black beans, rinsed and drained
1 11-ounce can whole kernel corn, drained
4 large tomatoes, chopped
1 avocado, peeled and chopped
1 large green bell pepper, chopped
1 bunch green onions, chopped
2 garlic cloves, chopped
1 large jalapeño pepper, chopped
1/3 cup fresh cilantro, chopped
1/4 cup fresh lime juice
2 tablespoons olive oil
1 teaspoon salt
2 teaspoons ground cumin

Combine all ingredients in a large bowl and toss gently. Cover and chill.
Makes 7 cups.

Cucumber Spread

. . . . . .

1 8-ounce package cream cheese, softened
2 to 3 tablespoons mayonnaise
Salt to taste
1 medium cucumber, peeled, seeded and grated
1/3 medium onion, grated
Bread slices

Mix all ingredients except bread slices together and chill for several hours.
Spread on bread slices, crusts trimmed.
Cut diagonally in fourths.
Makes 1 1/2 to 2 cups.

Bread

On our farm Dad raised corn, soybeans, wheat, oats and hay. In the fall Dad picked corn with a one-row corn picker pulled behind his red International Harvester tractor. A wagon to catch the corn was pulled behind the corn picker. One or two of us rode in the back of the wagon, and became buried to our chests in corn. Dad took time from his busy day to dig us out. When I was older, Dad had a modern two-row corn picker that mounted on his tractor. To make extra money when we were older we walked the cornfields to pick up the corn that the picker dropped. Dad paid us by the bushel.

During the summer Dad and the boys made hay and straw several times. Hay was made from clover and/or grass, and straw was made from wheat or oats. Hay was used to feed cattle; straw was used in the barn to bed-down the cattle and on the floor of the chicken house. Making hay and straw meant calling in the neighbors and hired men for help. The hay was made into bales in the field, picked up and loaded on a hay wagon (no sides on the wagon). The hay bales were taken to the outside of the barn, where a hayfork from the haymow, attached to a thick rope, would be lowered from a pulley to the wagon. The hayfork grabbed the bales and pulled the hay up into the mow through an opening in the second story of the barn. The men then released the bales from the fork and stacked the bales in the haymow. Back then the haymow was on the second floor of the barn. Mom and I would be busy fixing huge farm dinners for the men to eat at noon. This meant catching and cleaning a few chickens for fried chicken, cleaning many vegetables and lettuce from the garden and making bread, pies, cakes and cookies.

PHOTO ~ *Lawrence Perry*, my father

Egg Bread Loaves

. . . . . .

I've been making this bread for thirty years. It is a moist, tender and rich bread, and a family and company favorite. It is good toasted, and it freezes well.

1/4 cup sugar
1 tablespoon salt
1/4 cup butter
1 1/2 cups milk (I use half milk and half evaporated milk)
2 packages active dry yeast
1/2 cup warm water (110 to 115 degrees)
Pinch of sugar
3 eggs
7 to 7 1/2 cups all-purpose flour

Into a large bowl, put the 1/4 cup sugar, salt and butter. Scald the milk (heat until bubbles form around edge of pan) and pour into the large bowl, stirring until butter and sugar are dissolved. While milk mixture is cooling, in a small bowl dissolve yeast in water (put a pinch of sugar with the yeast and water). Let yeast mixture stand until foamy. Lightly beat eggs and add to sugar and butter mixture, along with the dissolved yeast and half the flour. Hand-mix until smooth. Add enough remaining flour to handle easily. (1 to 1 1/2 cups flour should remain for kneading.) Turn dough onto a floured surface; knead for 5 minutes, adding more flour as needed. Butter a large bowl and place dough in the bowl; lightly butter top of dough. Cover with a warm, dampened cotton towel, and let rise until double in size (about 1 1/4 to 1 1/2 hours). Punch down dough, lightly butter top of dough again and cover with a warm, dampened cotton towel. Let rise again until double in size (about 3/4 to 1 hour).

Punch down dough and divide into three equal portions. Shape loaves by flattening dough into a strip. Holding ends of strip, alternately slap and stretch dough until double the length of pan. Bring each end of strip to center, overlapping them slightly. Flatten dough evenly. With edge of hand, make lengthwise indentation in center of dough. Fold edges to center indentation; seal by pinching. Roll loaf to smooth. Place in pan, seam-side down. Butter tops. Cover with a warm, dampened cotton towel, and let rise until double in size (about 50 to 60 minutes).

Bake loaves in a 375° oven for 25 to 30 minutes or until bread sounds hollow when gently tapped. Remove from pans; butter top of each loaf, and cool on racks away from direct draft.

Makes 3 loaves.

Rosemary's Potato Rolls

. . . . . .

You will be a hit when you make potato rolls! They are moist, tender and flavorful.
Family and friends are glad when I place these rolls on the table or take them to gatherings.

1 cup milk
1/4 cup butter
1/4 cup sugar
1 teaspoon salt
3/4 cup mashed potatoes, unseasoned (packaged instant potatoes may be substituted)
1 package active dry yeast
1/4 cup warm water (110 to 115 degrees)
Pinch of sugar
4 to 4 1/2 cups all-purpose flour
1 egg, slightly beaten

Scald milk (heat in saucepan until bubbles form around edges). Add butter, the 1/4 cup sugar, salt and potatoes. Cool to lukewarm.

Sprinkle yeast on warm water, along with pinch of sugar; stir until dissolved. Let stand until foamy, about 5 to 10 minutes.

Combine milk mixture, yeast, 2 cups flour and the egg. Beat well by hand until dough is smooth and free of lumps. Stir in enough remaining flour, a little at a time, to make soft dough that leaves the sides of bowl.

Turn onto a lightly floured surface and knead until satiny and elastic, 5 to 10 minutes. Place in a lightly buttered bowl; turn dough over to butter top. Cover with a warm, dampened cotton towel and let rise in a warm place until double in size, 1 to 1 1/2 hours. Punch down. Turn onto work surface. Shape into a ball, cover and let rest 10 minutes. Divide into 40 to 48 equal portions and shape into walnut-size balls. Place two balls side by side in buttered muffin cups. Brush tops with melted butter. Cover with a warm, dampened cotton towel and let rise until almost doubled, about 1 hour.

Bake in a 375° oven for about 15 minutes. Place on a wire rack and brush tops with butter while hot. Makes about 2 dozen rolls.

Raisin Rye Bread

. . . . . .

The combination of raisins and rye gives this light rye bread a good flavor. The round loaves are attractive.

Sponge:
2 cups rye flour
1 package active dry yeast
Pinch of sugar
1 1/2 cups warm water (110 to 115 degrees)

Make a sponge by combining rye flour, yeast, pinch of sugar and 1 1/2 cups warm water. Blend into a light batter. Cover the bowl with plastic wrap and leave at room temperature until the sponge is bubbly, about 2 to 3 hours. It can be left up to 2 to 3 days to improve and strengthen the rye flavor.

Dough:
1/2 cup light raisins
1/2 cup dark raisins
1/3 cup water or brandy
1 tablespoon molasses
1 tablespoon vegetable oil
2 teaspoons salt
1/2 cup warm water
3 cups bread or all-purpose flour
1 egg plus 1 teaspoon milk, beaten together

Plump the raisins in the 1/3 cup water or brandy for 30 minutes. Drain, pat dry and set aside. Keep the brandy or water to add to the bread mixture.

In a small bowl, combine molasses, oil, salt and 1/2 cup warm water and pour into the sponge. Drop in the raisins and brandy.

Add flour to the sponge by hand or mixer. If the dough is soft and sticky, add liberal sprinkles of white flour.

Sprinkle the work surface with flour; turn out the dough and knead or use a dough hook to knead the dough until it is smooth and elastic (5 to 10 minutes).

Put the dough in a lightly buttered bowl and pat the surface of the dough with buttered fingers. Stretch a piece of plastic wrap tightly across the bowl. Leave the dough at room temperature until double in size (1 hour).

Punch down dough. Turn out onto work surface and divide into 2 pieces. Let rest for 5 minutes to relax dough.

(continued on next page)

Shape into round loaves, slightly flattened, or into oblong loaves. Place loaves on a baking sheet.
  Let rise 30 to 40 minutes.
Brush the loaves with the egg-milk mixture just before putting into the oven.
Bake in a 350° oven for 30 minutes.
Place on a wire rack to cool.
Makes 2 loaves.

Walnut Bread

. . . . . .

This bread has a nut flavor. You may want to serve it with a salad luncheon.

2 tablespoons honey
1 package active dry yeast
1 cup warm water (110 to 115 degrees)
Pinch of sugar
1 1/2 tablespoons walnut oil
1 teaspoon salt
1 1/2 cups whole-wheat flour
1 cup ground or finely chopped walnuts
1 1/2 cups all-purpose flour
1 egg
1 tablespoon water

In a large bowl, stir honey, yeast and pinch of sugar into warm water until dissolved. Let stand
  for about 5 to 10 minutes until foamy.
Add walnut oil and salt. Gradually stir in whole-wheat flour, ground walnuts and enough white flour
  to make soft dough.
Turn out on a floured surface. Knead until dough is smooth and elastic, about 8 minutes.
Turn dough over in a lightly buttered bowl. Cover with a warm, dampened cotton towel or cloth.
  Let rise for 1 1/4 to 1 1/2 hours until double in size.
Punch dough down; shape in a loaf. Place in buttered 9x5x3-inch loaf pan. Cover again with a warm,
  dampened cotton towel or cloth. Let rise for 45 minutes or until double in size. Whisk egg with
  1 tablespoon water. Brush over loaf.
Bake in a 350° oven for 30 to 35 minutes or until loaf sounds hollow when tapped.
Remove from pan. Cool on rack.
Makes 1 loaf.

Tomato-Cheese Bread

. . . . . .

3 tablespoons butter
1 1/2 teaspoons salt
1 cup tomato juice
3/4 cup warm water (110 to 115 degrees)
Pinch of sugar
2 packages active dry yeast
1 egg
1 1/2 cups (6 ounces) cheddar cheese, shredded
5 1/2 to 6 cups all-purpose flour

Place the butter and salt in a large bowl. Heat tomato juice until it starts to bubble.
    Add the warm tomato juice to the butter and salt, stirring until butter is melted.
In a small bowl, mix the warm water, pinch of sugar and the yeast. Let stand about 5 to 10 minutes,
    until foamy. Add to the tomato mixture; then add the egg, cheese and half the flour.
Mix until smooth. Stir in as much remaining flour as possible to make a soft dough. On a lightly
    floured surface, knead in as much remaining flour as possible until smooth and elastic, 6 to
    8 minutes. Shape into a ball. Place in a lightly buttered bowl and turn once. Cover with a warm,
    dampened cotton towel or cloth and let rise 1 hour or until double in size.
Punch down dough; divide in half. Cover with cloth; let rest 10 minutes.
Butter two 8x4-inch loaf pans. Shape each dough half into 1 loaf. Place in pans. Brush tops with
    melted butter; cover with a warm, dampened cotton cloth or towel. Let rise about 45 minutes
    or until nearly double in size.
Bake in a 375° oven for about 25 to 30 minutes or until loaves sound hollow when tapped.
Remove from pans. Cool on wire racks.
Makes 2 loaves.

Spiral Cinnamon-Raisin Bread

. . . . . .

I have made this yummy bread for many Sunday morning breakfasts. It is so attractive when sliced.

1/4 cup sugar
2 teaspoons salt

(continued on next page)

1/2 cup butter
1 1/2 cups raisins
1 1/2 cups milk
2 packages active dry yeast
1/2 cup warm water (110 to 115 degrees)
Pinch of sugar
3 eggs
7 1/2 cups all-purpose flour
1/2 cup sugar
2 teaspoons cinnamon
1/4 cup butter, melted

Place the 1/4 cup sugar, salt, the 1/2 cup butter and raisins into a large bowl. Scald the milk (heat until bubbles form around edge of pan) and pour into the large bowl, stirring until butter and sugar are dissolved. While milk mixture is cooling, in a small bowl, dissolve yeast in water (put a pinch of sugar with the yeast and water). Let yeast mixture stand until foamy. Lightly beat eggs and add to sugar and butter mixture, along with the dissolved yeast and half the flour. Hand-mix until smooth. Add enough remaining flour to handle easily. (1 to 1 1/2 cups flour should remain for kneading.)

Turn dough onto a floured surface; knead for 10 minutes, adding more flour as needed. Butter a large bowl, place dough in the bowl and lightly butter top of dough. Cover with a warm, dampened cotton towel and let rise until double in size (about 1 1/4 to 1 1/2 hours).

In a small bowl, mix 1/2 cup sugar and the cinnamon.

Turn dough out onto a lightly floured surface. Divide in half. Roll out one half into a 16x8-inch rectangle. Sprinkle with 3 tablespoons cinnamon-sugar, reserving the remainder. Starting at narrow end, roll up jellyroll fashion. Pinch edges and ends together to seal. Tuck ends under to give a smooth shape.

Place seam-side down in a buttered 9x5-inch loaf pan. Brush surface lightly with melted butter. Cover with a towel.

Repeat with other half of dough.

Let rise in a warm place until double in size (about 1 hour).

Brush each loaf with remaining melted butter, and sprinkle with remaining cinnamon-sugar.

Bake in a 375° oven for 35 to 40 minutes. Tops should be well browned and loaves should sound hollow when tapped. (If crust seems too brown after 25 minutes of baking, cover with foil.) Remove from pan immediately and cool slightly on a wire rack.

Serve warm.

Makes 2 loaves.

Honey Wheat Bread

. . . . . .

Delicious toasted!

2 packages active dry yeast
Pinch of sugar
1 1/2 cups warm water (110 to 115 degrees)
1 cup cottage cheese
1/2 cup honey
1/4 cup butter, melted
2 tablespoons sugar
1 tablespoon salt
1 egg, slightly beaten
4 to 5 cups all-purpose flour
3 cups whole-wheat flour

Stir yeast and pinch of sugar into warm water. Let stand until foamy, about 5 to 10 minutes.

In a large bowl, mix cottage cheese, honey, melted butter, the 2 tablespoons of sugar, salt and egg together. Add the yeast mixture, along with enough of both flours to make a firm dough. Knead on a well-floured surface for about 5 minutes.

Shape dough into a ball. Place in a lightly buttered bowl and turn once. Cover with a warm, dampened cotton towel or cloth; let rise 1 hour or until double in size (about 60 to 75 minutes).

Butter two 9x5-inch or 8x4-inch loaf pans.

Punch down dough, divide in half and shape into two loaves. Place into pans. Lightly butter tops of loaves. Cover with a warm, dampened cotton towel or cloth, and let rise until double in size (about 45 to 60 minutes).

Bake in a 350° oven for about 30 to 40 minutes. Remove from loaves from pans and cool on a wire rack.

Makes 2 loaves.

Black Pepper-Cheese Bread

. . . . . .

A different bread, and so good.

1/2 teaspoon dry mustard
1 teaspoon warm water
1 package active dry yeast
Pinch of sugar
1/4 cup warm water (110 to 115 degrees)
3/4 cup milk, scalded (heat until bubbles form around edge of pan)
1 1/2 teaspoons salt
1 teaspoon coarse black pepper
1 tablespoon sugar
1 tablespoon butter
1 egg, beaten
3 to 3 1/4 cups all-purpose flour
3/4 cup (3 ounces) cheddar cheese, shredded
Melted butter

In a small bowl dissolve mustard in 1 teaspoon water. Set aside.

In another small bowl sprinkle yeast and pinch of sugar over the 1/4 cup warm water. Stir to dissolve yeast and sugar. Let stand until foamy, about 5 to 10 minutes.

In a large bowl add the scalded milk to the salt, black pepper, the 1 tablespoon sugar and the 1 tablespoon butter. Stir to dissolve sugar and butter. Let cool to lukewarm. Add the mustard mixture, the yeast mixture and egg. Stir in half of the flour until smooth. Add the cheddar cheese and enough remaining flour to form a soft dough.

Turn dough out on a floured surface and knead for 5 minutes, adding more flour as needed to prevent sticking.

Place in a buttered bowl, turning once to butter surface. Cover with a warm, dampened cotton towel or cloth; let rise 1 to 1 1/2 hours or until doubled in size.

Punch down dough and shape into a loaf. Place in a buttered 9x5-inch loaf pan. Brush with melted butter. Cover and let rise in a warm place until double in size, about 45 to 60 minutes.

Bake in a 375° oven for 30 to 35 minutes or until bread sounds hollow when tapped.

Remove from pan; brush with melted butter and cool on rack.

Makes 1 loaf.

English Muffin Bread

. . . . . .

Like English muffins, try toasting this bread.

Cornmeal
2 packages active dry yeast
Pinch of sugar
1/2 cup warm water (110 to 115 degrees)
4 to 4 1/2 cups all-purpose flour
1/4 cup sugar
2 teaspoons salt
3/4 cup warm water
1/2 cup cooking oil
2 eggs, slightly beaten
Melted butter

Lightly grease two 8x4-inch loaf pans and sprinkle with cornmeal.
In a small bowl, sprinkle yeast and pinch of sugar over 1/2 cup warm water. Stir to dissolve sugar
    and yeast. Let stand until foamy, about 5 to 10 minutes.
In a large bowl, combine 1 1/2 cups flour, the 1/4 cup sugar, salt, 3/4 cup warm water, oil, eggs
    and yeast mixture. Stir until smooth. Stir in remaining 2 1/2 to 3 cups flour to form a stiff batter.
Cover dough with a warm, dampened cotton towel or cloth and let rise 1 hour or until double in size.
Stir batter vigorously for 30 seconds; spoon into prepared pans. Cover with cloth; let rise in
    warm place until double in size, about 30 to 45 minutes.
Bake in a 375° oven for 30 to 35 minutes or until loaves sound hollow when lightly tapped.
Remove from pans immediately; brush with melted butter and cool on wire racks.
Makes 2 loaves.

Anise Bread (Bread of the Dead)

. . . . . .

Marilyn says these special sweet loaves called "panes de muerto" are prepared to please the living (and the dead). They represent the animas or "souls" of the departed. They are oval or round.

Mix together:
1 1/2 cups all-purpose flour
1/2 cup sugar
1 teaspoon salt
1 tablespoon anise seed
2 packages dry yeast

Combine and heat in saucepan:
1/2 cup milk
1/2 cup water
1/2 cup butter

Set aside for later use:
4 eggs, slightly beaten
3 1/2 to 4 1/2 cups all-purpose flour

Glaze:
1/2 cup sugar
1/3 cup orange juice
2 tablespoons orange peel, grated

Mix dry ingredients, add warm liquid and beat until well mixed. Add 4 eggs and 1 cup flour and beat.
   Gradually blend in remaining 3 1/2 cups flour.
Knead on a lightly floured surface for 8 to 10 minutes.
Place dough in a greased bowl, cover with a dampened, warm cloth and let rise until double in size
   (1 1/2 hours).
Punch dough down and make into three oval or round loaves, placing on buttered cookie sheets.
   Cover and let rise again for 1 hour.
Bake in a 350° oven for 40 minutes.
Boil glaze ingredients for 2 minutes. Apply to warm loaves.
Makes 3 loaves.

Tomato Dinner Rolls

. . . . . .

These are very moist, flavorful, orange-colored rolls.

1 package active dry yeast
Pinch of sugar
1/4 cup warm water (110 to 115 degrees)
1 1/2 cups ripe tomatoes, peeled and finely chopped*
2 tablespoons sugar
2 tablespoons cooking oil
1 tablespoon snipped fresh herbs (parsley, basil or oregano)
    or 1 teaspoon dried herbs, crushed
1 1/2 teaspoons salt
4 to 4 1/2 cups all-purpose flour
1 beaten egg
1 tablespoon water

In a small bowl, sprinkle yeast and pinch of sugar over 1/4 cup warm water. Stir to dissolve sugar and yeast. Let stand until foamy, about 5 to 10 minutes.

In a large bowl, combine tomatoes, sugar, cooking oil, herbs and salt. Stir in the yeast mixture. Stir in 2 cups flour until smooth. Add 1 1/2 to 2 cups flour, stirring until a moderate soft dough forms.

Place in a buttered bowl, turning once to butter surface. Cover and chill for 2 to 24 hours.

Punch dough down. Divide in half. Cover and let rest for 10 minutes. Shape dough into golf-ball-size rolls. Tuck under and pinch seams on bottom.

Place about 2 inches apart on buttered baking sheets. Cover and let rise until double in size, about 45 to 60 minutes.

Brush tops with the beaten egg mixed with 1 tablespoon water.

Bake in a 375° oven for 12 to 15 minutes.

Makes 24 rolls.

*May substitute one 14 1/2-ounce can peeled Italian-style plum tomatoes for the fresh tomatoes. Drain canned tomatoes, reserving liquid. Chop tomatoes, then add enough reserved liquid to tomatoes to equal 1 1/2 cups.

Sweet Potato Rolls

. . . . .

Wonderful dinner rolls!

1 package active dry yeast
Pinch of sugar
1/4 cup warm water (110 to 115 degrees)
1/4 cup sugar
1 teaspoon salt
1/4 cup butter
3/4 cup fresh or canned sweet potatoes, mashed
3/4 cup milk, scalded (heat until bubbles form around edge of pan)
1 egg, beaten
3 1/2 to 4 cups all-purpose flour
Melted butter

In a small bowl, sprinkle yeast and pinch of sugar over 1/4 cup warm water. Stir to dissolve sugar
    and yeast. Let stand until foamy, about 5 to 10 minutes.
In a large bowl combine 1/4 cup sugar, salt, butter, and sweet potatoes. Stir in hot scalded milk
    until sugar is dissolved and butter is melted. Cool to lukewarm.
To the sweet potato mixture, add yeast mixture and egg. Stir in 2 cups flour until smooth.
    Add enough remaining flour to form a soft dough.
On a floured surface, knead dough until smooth and elastic, about 2 minutes.
Place in a buttered bowl, turning once to butter surface. Cover with a warm, dampened cotton
    towel or cloth; let rise in a warm place for 45 to 60 minutes or until double in size.
Butter 2 large cookie sheets. Punch down dough. On floured surface, toss dough lightly until no
    longer sticky. Divide dough into 18 pieces; shape into balls. Place 2 inches apart on buttered
    cookie sheets. Cover; let rise in a warm place until light and double in size, about 30 to 40 minutes.
Bake in a 375° oven for 15 to 20 minutes. Immediately remove from cookie sheets onto
    wire racks. Brush with melted butter.
Makes 18 rolls.

Sourdough French Bread

. . . . .

I cannot count the number of loaves I have made of this wonderful French bread.
Moist and tender on the inside, crunchy on the outside. Freezes well.

Starter Dough:
1/4 cup milk
1/2 cup water
2 teaspoons vegetable oil
1 package active dry yeast
Pinch of sugar
1/4 cup warm water (110 to 115 degrees)
2 teaspoons sugar
1 1/2 teaspoons salt
2 1/3 cups all-purpose flour

Combine milk, water and oil; bring to boil. Cool to lukewarm.
In a small bowl, sprinkle yeast and pinch of sugar over 1/4 cup warm water. Stir to dissolve sugar
    and yeast. Let stand until foamy, about 5 to 10 minutes.
Add yeast mixture to milk mixture along with sugar and salt. Add flour and stir just enough to
    blend thoroughly. Cover; let stand in a warm place for 12 to 18 hours to sour. (Recipe makes
    enough starter for about 12 loaves. Remaining starter can be stored tightly covered in refrigerator
    for several days. Measure amount needed and bring to room temperature before using.)

Bread:
1/2 cup milk
1 cup water
1 1/2 tablespoons vegetable oil
1 package active dry yeast
Pinch of sugar
1/4 cup warm water (110 to 115 degrees)
1 1/2 tablespoons sugar
2 1/2 teaspoons salt
4 3/4 cups all-purpose flour
2 tablespoons Starter Dough
1 egg white
1 tablespoon cold water

(continued on next page)

Combine milk, water and oil; bring to boil. Cool to lukewarm.

In a small bowl, sprinkle yeast and pinch of sugar over 1/4 cup warm water. Stir to dissolve sugar and yeast. Let stand until foamy, about 5 to 10 minutes.

Add yeast mixture, the 1 1/2 tablespoons sugar and salt to cooled milk mixture. Place flour in a large bowl; pour milk into well made in center of flour. Add starter and blend well. DO NOT KNEAD. Place in a buttered bowl, turning once to butter surface. Cover with a warm, dampened cotton towel or cloth; let rise in a warm place for 60 minutes or until double in size.

Turn onto a lightly floured surface. DO NOT KNEAD. Divide in half. Roll each half into a 15x10-inch rectangle. Roll up tightly toward you, beginning at wide end; seal edges. With hand on each end, roll to taper ends slightly. Place on a baking sheet covered with heavy foil. (Pleat foil between loaves.) With a sharp knife, make cuts about 1/8 inch deep diagonally along loaf, about 2 inches apart.

Let rise, uncovered, in a warm place until a little more than double in size, about 1 hour.

Bake in a 425° oven for 15 minutes.

Reduce heat to 350°. Bake 15 to 20 minutes longer.

Remove from oven. Brush top and sides of loaves with 1 egg white mixed with 1 tablespoon cold water.

Bake 5 minutes longer. Cool on a wire rack.

Makes 2 loaves.

Whole-Wheat Raisin Loaf

. . . . .

Try serving toasted with jam or jelly. Makes wonderful French toast.

2 packages active dry yeast
Pinch of sugar
3/4 cup warm water (110 to 115 degrees)
1/2 cup sugar
3 teaspoons salt
1 teaspoon cinnamon
1/2 teaspoon nutmeg
2 cups milk
1/4 cup cooking oil
3 1/2 to 4 cups all-purpose flour
3 cups whole-wheat flour
1 cup rolled oats
1 cups raisins
Melted butter
Sugar, if desired

In a small bowl, sprinkle yeast and pinch of sugar over 1/4 cup warm water. Stir to dissolve sugar
    and yeast. Let stand until foamy, about 5 to 10 minutes.
In a large bowl, combine the 1/2 cup sugar, salt, cinnamon and nutmeg. In a small saucepan
    heat milk, remaining 1/2 cup warm water and 1/4 cup oil until very warm (bubbles will form
    around edge of pan).
Pour hot milk mixture in with sugar mixture. Stir until sugar is dissolved. Add 1 1/2 cups
    all-purpose flour and stir until smooth. Stir in whole-wheat flour, rolled oats, raisins and
    an additional 1 to 1 1/2 cups all-purpose flour until dough pulls cleanly away from sides of bowl.
On a floured surface, knead in 1/2 to 3/4 cup all-purpose flour until dough is smooth and elastic,
    about 5 minutes. Place in a buttered bowl, turning once to butter surface. Cover with a warm,
    dampened cotton towel or cloth; let rise in a warm place for 45 to 60 minutes or until double
    in size.
Punch down dough. Divide dough into 2 parts; shape into loaves. Place in buttered 9x5-inch loaf
    pans; brush tops with melted butter. Cover; let rise in a warm place until light and double in size,
    about 45 minutes.
Bake in a 375° oven for 40 minutes or until loaves sound hollow when lightly tapped. Cover
    with foil last 10 minutes of baking if necessary to avoid excessive browning. Remove from pans
    onto a wire rack. Brush tops of loaves with melted butter, and sprinkle with sugar, if desired.
Makes 2 loaves.

Breakfast Breads

Dad and Mom milked by hand our  own herd of six or seven cows. Milking, tending and feeding the farm animals were finished before breakfast. Often up in the morning at five, they sat on one-legged stools in the barn stalls to do the milking by hand (no milking machines). While sitting on their stools milking, they watched for cows that decided to kick, and for a cow's flying tail swatting flies from its large, bulky body. Dad got his first electric milking machine the night my brother Jim was born. With such a modern convenience, Dad enlarged his herd. The first cows were holsteins, guernsey and jerseys. The milk from these cows was sold in ten-gallon cans. In years following, we had a Jersey cow for just our family's needs.

There always was plenty of whole milk to drink. The cream, skimmed from the top of the milk (milk was not homogenized in those days), was used to make butter. Churning butter by hand in the gallon glass churn with its wood paddles and metal hand crank is one of the first family duties I remember doing. After removing the butter from the churned cream, the milk left from the butter was buttermilk. Any extra cream was made into sour cream. Mom left the cream at room temperature covered with cheesecloth until it soured. The extra milk was made into cottage cheese. The quality and flavors of Mom's own homemade butter, sour cream and cottage cheese now seem to be in the past.

PHOTO ~ *Celestine and Mary Brucker, my mother's grandparents*

Sweet Roll Dough (basic recipe)

. . . . .

When making yeast sweet rolls, this is the basic dough recipe I've used since I was eleven years old. To this day, I have not found a better recipe.

1 1/2 cups milk, scalded (I use half milk and half evaporated milk)
1/2 cup sugar
2 teaspoons salt
1/2 cup butter
2 packages active dry yeast
1/2 cup warm water (110 to 115 degrees)
Pinch of sugar
2 eggs
7 to 7 1/2 cups all-purpose flour

In a saucepan, scald milk (bubbles will form around side of pan). Place the sugar, salt and butter in a large bowl. Add the scalded milk; stir until the sugar is dissolved and the butter is melted. Cool to lukewarm.

Meanwhile, in a small bowl dissolve the yeast in the 1/2 cup warm water, adding the pinch of sugar. Let stand until foamy.

Add the eggs and the dissolved yeast to the milk mixture. Add half of the flour and mix with a spoon until smooth. Add enough remaining flour to handle easily. Turn onto a lightly floured surface; knead until smooth (about 5 minutes).

Shape the dough into a ball. Place dough in a buttered bowl, turning once to grease surface of the dough. Cover with a warm, dampened cotton cloth. Let rise in a warm place until double in size, about 1 1/2 hours. Punch down dough. Let rise again until almost double in size, about 45 minutes.

Use dough to make sweet rolls in the following six bread recipes.

Cinnamon Rolls

. . . . . .

Use 1/2 of the Sweet Roll Dough (see recipe, page 42).

Roll dough into a 15x9-inch rectangle. Spread with 3 to 4 tablespoons *melted butter*, and sprinkle
with mixture of 1/2 cup *sugar* and 2 teaspoons *cinnamon.*
If desired, add 1/2 cup *chopped nuts* such as pecans.
Roll dough up tightly, beginning at a wide side. Seal well by pinching edges of roll together.
Even up roll by stretching slightly.
Cut roll into 1-inch slices. Place in a buttered 13x9-inch pan or 18 buttered muffin cups.
Cover with a warm, dampened cotton towel. Let rise until double in size, about 45 to 60 minutes.
Bake in a 375° oven for 20 to 25 minutes. While still warm, drizzle White Glaze (see recipe, page 51)
over rolls. Freezes well.
Makes 15 rolls.

Tea Ring

. . . . . .

Use 1/2 of the Sweet Roll Dough (see recipe, page 42).

Roll dough into a 15x9-inch rectangle. Spread with 3 to 4 tablespoons melted *butter* and sprinkle
with mixture of 1/2 cup *sugar* and 2 teaspoons *cinnamon.*
If desired, add 1/2 cup *chopped nuts* such as pecans.
Roll dough up tightly, beginning at a wide side. Seal well by pinching edges of roll together.
Even up roll by stretching slightly.
Place on a buttered cookie sheet; form dough into a circle, sealed-side down, and pinch
ends together. Using scissors, make cuts 2/3 of the way through the ring at 1-inch intervals.
Turn each section on its side. Cover with a warm, dampened cotton towel.
Bake in a 375° oven for 20 to 25 minutes.
While still warm, drizzle White Glaze (see recipe, page 51) over tea ring. Freezes well.
Serves 6 to 8.

Bohemian Braid

. . . . . .

Use all of the Sweet Roll Dough recipe; do not divide.

Sweet Roll Dough (see recipe, page 42)
2 teaspoons grated lemon rind
1/4 teaspoon mace
1 cup raisins
1 cup blanched almonds, chopped
Red candied cherries
Pecan halves

Make Sweet Roll Dough recipe, except, with first addition of flour, add lemon rind, mace,
    raisins and almonds.
After dough rises, divide dough into 2 portions to make 2 braids. Divide each portion into
    4 equal parts. Shape 3 of the parts into 14-inch strands. Place on a lightly buttered baking sheet.
    Braid loosely, fastening strands at one end; tuck ends under.
Divide fourth part of dough into 3 pieces and shape each into 12-inch-long strands. Braid these
    3 strands and place the small braid on top of large braid.
Make another double braid from second portion of dough.
Cover with a warm, dampened cotton towel and let rise until double in size, about 45 to 60 minutes.
Bake in a 350° oven for 25 to 30 minutes.
While still warm, drizzle with White Glaze (see recipe, page 51). Decorate with red candied cherries
    and pecan halves. Freezes well.
Makes 2 braids.

Orange Rolls

. . . . . .

Make Sweet Roll Dough (see recipe, page 42); divide dough in half. Roll each dough half into a 16x8-inch rectangle.

Filling:
1 cup sugar
1/2 cup (1 stick) butter, melted
4 tablespoons grated orange peel
1/2 cup pecans, chopped (*optional*)

Prepare filling by stirring together all filling ingredients. Spread half of filling on each dough rectangle. Roll up dough, starting with long side, jelly-roll style. Seal edges. Cut crosswise into 1-inch slices. Place rolls, cut-side down, in four buttered 9-inch square baking pans or two 13x9-inch baking pans, or muffin tins.
Cover with a warm, dampened, cotton towel. Let rise until double in size, about 45 to 60 minutes.
Bake in a 375° oven for 20 to 25 minutes.
Remove from pan and drizzle with Orange Glaze (see recipe, below).
Makes 16 rolls.

Orange Glaze

. . . . . .

Place 1 cup *confectioner's sugar* into a bowl, adding enough *orange juice* to make an icing of drizzling consistency. Drizzle over warm breads.
Makes about 1/3 cup.

Caramel-Pecan Rolls

. . . . . .

For caramel rolls with a different twist, use hickory nuts (you will have to crack your own; you cannot buy them) instead of pecans. What a delicious difference! Since my two children were born, it's been a family tradition to serve Caramel-Pecan Rolls using hickory nuts on Christmas morning. Now they bring my grandchildren on Christmas morning to enjoy them. The rolls bake while we open gifts.

1 cup brown sugar, packed
1/2 cup butter, melted
2 tablespoons corn syrup
1 to 1 1/2 cups pecan halves or pieces
Sweet Roll Dough (see recipe, page 42)
4 tablespoon butter, softened
1/2 cup granulated sugar
1 teaspoon cinnamon

In a saucepan, combine brown sugar, melted butter and corn syrup. Cook and stir just until blended. Distribute evenly into 3 well-buttered 9-inch round or square layer pans. Top mixture with pecans.

Roll dough to a 24x9-inch rectangle. Spread with softened butter.

Combine the 1/2 cup granulated sugar and the cinnamon; sprinkle over dough. Roll up, jelly-roll style, beginning with a long side; seal edges.

Cut into 1-inch slices. Place rolls, cut-side down, in prepared pans. Cover with a warm, dampened cotton towel. Let rise until double in size, about 45 to 60 minutes.

Bake in a 375° oven for 20 to 25 minutes. Invert on wire racks or plates.

Freezes well.

Makes 24 rolls.

Apricot Streusel Coffee Cake

. . . . . .

Wonderful to give at Christmas! (Keep one for yourself.)

1 11-ounce package dried apricots, coarsely chopped
2/3 cup light brown sugar, firmly packed
1 1/4 cup water
1 cup walnuts, chopped
2 tablespoons fresh lemon juice
2 tablespoons butter
2 tablespoons granulated sugar
1/3 cup all-purpose flour
1/2 teaspoon ground cinnamon
Sweet Roll Dough (see recipe, page 42)
1 egg yolk
2 tablespoons milk

Combine apricots, light brown sugar, water, walnuts and lemon juice in a saucepan. Place over moderate heat and bring to a boil, stirring constantly. Reduce heat to moderately low and continue cooking 5 minutes, stirring constantly. Remove from heat and cool.

Place butter, granulated sugar, flour and cinnamon in a bowl and mix together until crumbly. Set aside to use as topping.

Divide Sweet Roll Dough in half.

Roll each dough half into a 16x8-inch rectangle. Place each rectangle on a buttered cookie sheet. Spoon half of the apricot filling lengthwise down the center of each rectangle. With a knife, cut strips about 1 inch wide from edge of filling to outer edge of dough. Fold strips at an angle across filling, alternating from side to side. Cover and let rise in a warm place for 1 hour, or until double in size.

Mix egg yolk and milk together and brush over cakes. Sprinkle with reserved crumb mixture.

Bake in a 350° oven for 25 to 30 minutes. Remove from cookie sheets and cool on wire racks.

Freezes well.

Makes 2 coffee cakes.

Sugared Golden Puffs

. . . . . .

My mother, Mary Jane Perry, is well known for her sugared golden puffs. These puffs resemble doughnut holes. It's a recipe that has come down through the family. With eight children, Mom had to make a double batch. They are quick to make and, served warm, you will receive numerous compliments.

2 cups all-purpose flour
1/4 cup sugar
3 teaspoons baking powder
1 teaspoon salt
1/2 teaspoon nutmeg
1 egg, beaten
3/4 cup milk
1/4 cup vegetable oil
Vegetable oil for deep-frying

In a medium bowl, stir together all dry ingredients.
In a separate small bowl, stir together all liquid ingredients. Pour liquids into dry ingredients
    and stir with a fork until thoroughly mixed.
Drop by rounded teaspoons into hot (375°) vegetable shortening or oil for deep-frying.
    Fry a few puffs at a time until golden brown on all sides, about 3 minutes. (Don't fry too many
    puffs at a time or they will become soaked with grease.) Drain puffs on a wire rack or paper towels.
Roll in Cinnamon-Sugar (see recipe, below) or dip into White Glaze (see recipe, page 51).
Makes 48 to 50 puffs.

Cinnamon-Sugar

. . . . . .

Mix together 1/2 cup *granulated sugar* and 1 teaspoon *cinnamon.*
Makes 1/2 cup.

German Sour Cream Twists

. . . . . .

Another recipe from my mother, who made these delicate, sugary twists while I was growing up. Watch out! They do not last long.

1 package active dry yeast
1/4 cup warm water (110 to 115 degrees)
Pinch of sugar
3 1/2 cups all-purpose flour
1 teaspoon salt
1 cup (2 sticks) butter, at room temperature
3/4 cup sour cream
1 whole egg, beaten
2 egg yolks, beaten
1 teaspoon vanilla
1 cup sugar

In a small bowl, dissolve the yeast in the 1/4 cup warm water, adding the pinch of sugar. Let stand until foamy.

Stir flour and salt together in a large bowl. Cut in butter until it resembles fine crumbs.

Add dissolved yeast, sour cream, whole egg, egg yolks and vanilla to the flour mixture. Mix well with a spoon. Cover with a damp cloth and refrigerate for 2 hours.

Divide dough in half. Roll each half on a sugared surface to an 8x16-inch rectangle. Fold ends to center, overlapping ends. Sprinkle with sugar; roll again to same size. Repeat a third time.

Roll to about 1/4 inch thick. Cut into 1x4-inch strips. Twist ends in opposite directions, stretching dough slightly. Place on an unbuttered baking sheet, pressing ends down.

Bake in a 375° oven for 12 to 15 minutes. Remove from baking sheet immediately and let cool on a wire rack. Freezes well.

Makes 32 twists.

Cinnamon Twists

. . . . . .

Mom would usually make Cinnamon Twists at the same time she made German Sour Cream Twists (see recipe, page 49). With all of us at home, these delicacies did not last long.

1 package active dry yeast
1/4 cup warm water (110 to 115 degrees)
Pinch of sugar
3/4 cup sour cream
3 tablespoons granulated sugar
1/8 teaspoon baking soda
1 teaspoon salt
1 egg, beaten
2 tablespoons butter, melted
3 cups all-purpose flour
2 tablespoons butter, softened
1/3 cup brown sugar, firmly packed
1 teaspoon cinnamon

In a small bowl, dissolve the yeast in the 1/4 cup warm water, adding the pinch of sugar.
   Let stand until foamy.
In a saucepan, heat sour cream to lukewarm. Stir in the granulated sugar, baking soda and salt.
   Add the egg, melted butter and dissolved yeast.
In a large bowl, mix the liquid ingredients with the 3 cups flour. Mix well with a spoon.
Turn dough onto a floured surface; knead several times until it is smooth. Roll to a 24x6-inch
   rectangle. Spread dough with the softened butter. Combine brown sugar and cinnamon. Sprinkle
   half of dough lengthwise with the brown sugar and cinnamon mixture. Fold other half over.
Cut into 1-inch-wide strips. Hold strips at both ends and twist. Place on a buttered baking sheet;
   press ends down. Let rise for about 1 hour.
Bake in a 375° oven for 12 to 15 minutes. Remove from baking sheet immediately to a wire rack.
   While still hot, drizzle with White Glaze (see recipe, page 51).
Makes 24 twists.

White Glaze

. . . . . .

Often used to ice warm sweet rolls and breads.

Place 1 cup *confectioner's sugar* and 1/2 teaspoon *vanilla flavoring* into a small bowl, adding enough milk
   or cream to make an icing of drizzling consistency.
Makes 1/3 cup.

Egg Pancakes

. . . . . .

*My mother would fix flat, thin egg pancakes for supper or for breakfast for eight children. Of course, she
would have three iron skillets going at once, trying to keep up with eight hungry kids. She would always have
a big bowl of homemade applesauce, either fresh or canned, made from transparent apples to spoon on top
of the pancakes. We would alternate putting applesauce or syrup on them. Mom got her recipe from Dad's
mother. Today, these thin pancakes are called French crepes.*

1 cup milk
3 eggs, well beaten
3/4 cup sifted all-purpose flour
1 tablespoon sugar
1/4 teaspoon salt

Beat milk into well-beaten eggs. Sift together flour, sugar and salt into milk mixture. Beat with
   a rotary beater or electric mixer until batter is smooth.
Over medium heat, pour about 4 or more tablespoons batter into a lightly buttered 8-inch skillet.
Bake until light golden brown on both sides, turning once. Repeat, buttering skillet for each pancake.
Makes about 8 pancakes.

Sour Cream Pancakes

. . . . . .

The addition of sour cream makes light, fluffy pancakes with a great flavor. They were a favorite of Mike and Lesly while growing up. (A half-cup of blueberries may be folded into batter—what a treat!)

1 cup all-purpose flour
3 teaspoons baking powder
1/4 teaspoon salt
1 tablespoon sugar
1 egg
1 cup milk
1/3 cup dairy sour cream
2 tablespoons butter, melted
Butter and maple syrup

In a medium bowl sift together flour, baking powder, salt and sugar.
Beat together egg, milk and sour cream.
Pour milk mixture over dry ingredients and blend with a fork until batter is just smooth.
   Stir in butter.
Pour 2 to 3 tablespoons batter onto a hot skillet or griddle. Brown on one side until golden.
   Turn and brown on the other side. If cakes brown too fast, lower heat. Serve hot with butter
   and maple syrup.
Makes 8 to 10 pancakes.

Baked Porridge

. . . . . .

Joyce, my sister-in-law in Evansville, served this for breakfast to the Perry clan during the Christmas holidays. Needless to say, when we heard she was serving "porridge," several Perry noses wrinkled. But when the porridge was served, most everyone was asking for the recipe, including myself. It is very good, and a perfect choice for holiday breakfasts.

3 cups water
3/4 teaspoon salt
1 2/3 cups old-fashioned oats
2/3 cups raisins
1/3 cup maple syrup
1/4 cup dark molasses
1/4 cup brown sugar, firmly packed
1/4 cup walnuts, chopped
2 eggs, slightly beaten
1/2 teaspoon cinnamon
1/2 teaspoon ginger
1/4 teaspoon nutmeg
Milk

Bring water and salt to boil in a medium saucepan. Cook oats at a medium-low temperature for 5 minutes, stirring frequently. Transfer to a 6-cup casserole dish. Add all remaining ingredients and stir until combined.
Bake in a 350° oven for 1 hour.
Serve with milk.
Serves 6.

Blueberry Tea Loaf

. . . . . .

2 1/2 cups sifted all-purpose flour
2 teaspoons baking powder
1/4 teaspoon nutmeg
1/4 teaspoon salt
1/2 cup butter, softened
1 cup sugar
2 eggs
1 cup milk
1 cup fresh blueberries or 1 cup frozen blueberries, thawed and well drained
Confectioner's sugar

Stir flour together with baking powder, nutmeg and salt; set aside.

In a large bowl, with an electric mixer at high speed, beat butter with sugar and eggs until light and fluffy, about 2 minutes.

At low speed, beat in flour mixture (in fourths) alternately with milk (in thirds), beginning and ending with flour mixture. Beat just until smooth.

Gently fold in blueberries just until combined.

Turn into a buttered 9x5-inch loaf pan.

Bake in a 350° oven for 60 to 65 minutes or until a cake tester inserted in center comes out clean. Let cool in pan on a wire rack for 20 minutes. Remove from pan onto wire rack; sprinkle top with confectioner's sugar.

Makes 1 loaf.

Apple-Nut Bread

. . . . . .

1/2 cup butter, softened
1 cup sugar
2 eggs
2 tablespoons sour cream
2 cups all-purpose flour
1 teaspoon baking powder
1 teaspoon baking soda
1/2 teaspoon salt
1 cup chopped pecans
1 cup unpeeled apples, grated

Beat butter and sugar together until light and fluffy. Add eggs, one at a time, beating well after each.
   Blend in sour cream.
Stir together dry ingredients; add nuts. Combine with butter-sugar mixture. Stir in apples. Pour into
   a buttered 9x5-inch loaf pan.
Bake in a 325° oven for 50 to 60 minutes or until a toothpick inserted in center comes out clean.
Cool on a wire rack for 10 minutes; remove from pan.
Makes 1 loaf.

Sour Cream-Blueberry-Banana Bread

. . . . . .

A wonderful, moist, flavorful bread.

2 cups all-purpose flour
1 teaspoon baking soda
1/2 teaspoon salt
1/2 teaspoon cinnamon
1 cup butter, softened
3/4 cup sugar
2 large eggs
2 medium-size ripe bananas, mashed (about 1 cup)
1/2 cup sour cream
1 cup fresh blueberries
1/2 cup pecans, coarsely chopped

In a bowl, stir together flour, baking soda, salt and cinnamon. Set aside

In a large bowl, cream butter and sugar until light and fluffy. Add eggs, bananas and sour cream; beat until blended. Gradually beat in dry ingredients at low speed and continue beating just until smooth. Fold in blueberries and pecans.

Pour batter into a buttered 9x5-inch loaf pan.

Bake in a 350° oven for 50 to 60 minutes or until a toothpick inserted in center comes out clean. Let cool in pan.

Makes 1 loaf.

Date, Walnut and Brazil Nut Loaves

. . . . . .

A *different nut bread that makes a wonderful gift through the holidays. It will keep for a long time.*

1 1/2 cups all-purpose flour
1 1/2 cups sugar
1 teaspoon baking powder
1 teaspoon salt
2 pounds seedless dates, cut up
1 pound shelled walnuts, chopped
1 pound shelled Brazil nuts, chopped
1 jar (8 ounces) maraschino cherries, well drained
5 extra-large eggs, beaten
1 teaspoon vanilla

In a large bowl stir together flour, sugar, baking powder and salt. Add the dates, walnuts, brazil nuts and maraschino cherries. Stir in the beaten eggs and vanilla. Mix well.
Pour into 2 buttered 9x5-inch loaf pans.
Bake in a 325° oven for 50 to 60 minutes or until a toothpick inserted in center comes out clean.
Cool in pans, then remove. Wrap cooled loaves in foil and refrigerate. Will keep 2 to 3 months in refrigerator.
Makes 2 loaves.

Buttermilk-Carrot Bread

. . . . . .

1 1/2 cups all-purpose flour
1 cup sugar
1 teaspoon baking soda
1/4 teaspoon salt
1 teaspoon cinnamon
2 eggs
1/2 cup buttermilk
1/2 cup oil
1 teaspoon vanilla
1 cup carrots, shredded

In a large bowl mix together the flour, sugar, baking soda, salt and cinnamon.

In a small bowl stir together the eggs, buttermilk, oil and vanilla. Add to flour mixture. Fold in the shredded carrots.

Butter bottom of a 9x5-inch loaf pan. Spoon in batter.

Bake in a 350° oven for 50 to 60 minutes.

Makes 1 loaf.

Muffins

Wash day for our large farm family was usually twice a week, with eight to ten loads each time. Clothes were washed in an old wringer-washer. A hose was used to put water in the washer. After washing, we removed the clothes with a long wooden stick and put them through a wringer (we had to watch our fingers). From the wringer, the clothes dropped into the first of two washtubs filled with water. By hand we dipped the clothes in and out of the water to remove the soap. The load went through the wringer and dropped into the second tub of water. Once again, we rinsed the clothes in the water and sent them through the final wringer. Finally we hung the wash outside during decent weather with wooden clothespins. On rainy days or in the winter we hung them to dry on lines in the basement. Hanging clothes and the many diapers to dry meant shaking each to shake out some of the wrinkles before putting on the clothesline. With all the babies in diapers, the lines were filled more than once with diapers to dry. A breezy day meant clothes dried faster; they were removed, with the next basket of wet clothes ready to hang. (No!! We didn't have clothes dryers in those days.)

Ironing the clothes was quite a chore back then. After the wash was dry, the items that needed ironing (which was about everything, except for the towels and washcloths) were sprinkled with water, rolled up tight, put in a clean wood bushel basket and covered with a damp towel. We needed a bushel basket due to our large family. The dampened clothes had to sit for a few hours before ironing them. Dampening the clothes helped to remove the wrinkles when they were ironed. We would spend a whole day or more ironing. Mom made her own starch with powder from a box. The brand we used was Argo Laundry Starch. Mom mixed the powdered starch with cold water in a pan, added boiling water and brought it to a boil, until it was the correct stiffness. Crocheted doilies, shirt collars and anything that needed a heavy starch were dipped in the starch mixture. To make a lighter starch for aprons and tablecloths, Mom thinned the starch with cool water. (No!! We didn't have spray starch in those days, either.)

PHOTO ~ *Lawrence Jr., Jim, Mick, myself and Albert,* myself and my brothers

French Breakfast Muffins

. . . . . .

My daughter, Lesly, won reserve champion for these muffins at the county 4-H Fair the summer of 1988. The flavor and texture are excellent.

1 1/2 cups plus 2 tablespoons all-purpose flour
3/4 cup sugar
2 teaspoons baking powder
1/4 teaspoon salt
1/4 teaspoon ground nutmeg
1/2 cup milk
1 egg, beaten with 1/3 cup butter, melted

Topping:
1/3 cup butter, melted
1/2 cup sugar
1 teaspoon ground cinnamon
1/2 teaspoon vanilla

Line muffin pan with 10 paper baking cups, or butter and flour muffin tins.
Combine the first 5 ingredients in a large bowl. Add milk and the egg-butter mixture, and mix.
Fill muffin cups 1/2 full.
Bake in a 400° oven for 15 to 20 minutes.
Remove from pan. Dip muffin tops in melted butter. Roll tops in mixture of sugar, cinnamon and vanilla, and set on rack. Serve warm. These muffins freeze beautifully.
Makes 10 to 12 muffins.

Blueberry Muffins

. . . . . .

I've made these blueberry muffins countless times the past 35 years. You can't resist them. The first morning after picking fresh blueberries I make a batch. They don't stand a chance of cooling before they are gone. There is absolutely no comparison between fresh blueberry muffins and store-bought, or from a box mix.

1 egg
1/2 cup milk
1/4 cup butter, melted
1 1/2 cups all-purpose flour
1/2 cup sugar
2 teaspoons baking powder
1/2 teaspoon salt
1 1/4 cups fresh blueberries or 1 1/4 cups frozen blueberries, thawed

Butter 10 muffin cups or line with paper baking cups.

In a medium bowl beat egg with a fork. Stir in milk and melted butter.

In a large bowl blend together dry ingredients. Stir the egg mixture into the dry ingredients just until flour is moistened. Batter should be lumpy. Do not overmix. Gently fold in blueberries.

Fill muffin cups 2/3 full.

Bake in a 400° oven for 20 to 25 minutes.

Makes 10 muffins.

Lemon-Poppy Seed Muffins

3 cups all-purpose flour
1 1/2 teaspoons baking soda
1 1/2 teaspoons baking powder
1/2 teaspoon salt
3/4 cup unsalted butter, softened
1 cup plus 2 tablespoons sugar
3 eggs
1 cup sour cream
1/3 cup fresh lemon juice
1 1/2 teaspoons vanilla
1/4 cup poppy seeds
1 teaspoon grated lemon zest
Sugar to garnish

In a medium bowl sift together the flour, baking soda, baking powder and salt. Set aside.
In large mixing bowl cream butter and 1 cup plus 2 tablespoons sugar with an electric mixer
at medium speed until fluffy, scraping bowl often. Add eggs, one at a time, beating well after
each addition.
Add flour mixture alternately with sour cream, lemon juice and vanilla; beat at low speed until
blended. Fold in poppy seeds and lemon zest.
Fill muffin cups lined with paper baking cups 2/3 full. Sprinkle tops with additional sugar.
Bake in a 375° oven for 18 to 20 minutes.
Makes 30 muffins.

Garden Herb Muffins

. . . . . .

2 cups all-purpose flour
2 tablespoons sugar
1 tablespoon baking powder
1/4 teaspoon salt
1 3-ounce package cream cheese
3/4 cup milk
1/2 cup carrots, finely shredded or grated
1/3 cup green onions, chopped
1/4 cup vegetable oil
1 egg

Butter 12 muffin cups or line with paper baking cups.

In a large bowl combine flour, sugar, baking powder and salt. Cut in cream cheese with a pastry blender until mixture resembles fine crumbs.

In a small bowl combine milk, carrots, green onions, oil and egg until blended. Stir into flour mixture just until moistened.

Spoon evenly into prepared muffin cups.

Bake in a 400° oven 25 to 30 minutes. Cool on a wire rack for 10 minutes before serving.

Makes 12 muffins.

Apple-Walnut Muffins

. . . . .

Try serving these tasty muffins on a fall or winter morning.

2 cups all-purpose flour
2 teaspoons baking powder
1 1/2 teaspoons ground cinnamon
1/4 teaspoon ground nutmeg
1/4 teaspoon salt
2 eggs, beaten
2/3 cup frozen unsweetened apple juice concentrate, thawed
1/3 cup butter, melted
1 teaspoon vanilla
1 cup peeled apples, finely chopped
1/2 cup walnuts, chopped

Butter 12 muffin cups or line with paper baking cups.
Combine dry ingredients in a medium bowl. In a small bowl combine eggs, apple juice concentrate, butter and vanilla until blended. Stir into flour mixture just until moistened. Stir in apples and walnuts.
Spoon batter into prepared cups, filling each cup 3/4 full.
Bake in a 350° oven 25 minutes or until golden brown. Cool in pan 5 minutes.
Makes 12 muffins.

Sun-dried Tomato Muffins

. . . . . .

Great for a luncheon.

1 cup all-purpose flour
1/2 cup whole-wheat flour
2 teaspoons baking powder
2 teaspoons sugar
1/2 teaspoon pepper
1/4 teaspoon salt
1 cup milk
1/4 cup vegetable oil
1 egg
4 to 6 tablespoons chopped green olives *(optional)*
2 tablespoons chopped oil-packed sun-dried tomatoes, drained

Butter 12 muffin cups or line with paper baking cups.
Combine dry ingredients in a medium bowl. In a small bowl whisk together milk, oil and egg.
   Add to dry ingredients, mixing just until moistened. Gently stir in olives and tomatoes.
Spoon batter into prepared muffin cups.
Bake in a 425° oven 15 minutes.
Makes 12 muffins.

Cheddar-Raisin Muffins

. . . . .

2 cups all-purpose flour
3 1/2 teaspoons baking powder
1/2 teaspoon salt
1 teaspoon paprika
1/4 cup butter
1 cup (4 ounces) cheddar cheese, shredded
2/3 cup raisins
1 egg, beaten
1 cup milk

Butter and flour 12 muffin cups or line with paper baking cups.
Combine first 4 ingredients in a large bowl; cut in butter with a pastry blender until mixture
    resembles coarse crumbs. Stir in cheese and raisins. Make a well in center of mixture.
In a small bowl combine egg and milk; add to dry ingredients, stirring just until moistened.
Spoon batter into muffin cups.
Bake in a 425° oven 20 to 25 minutes.
Makes 12 to 14 muffins.

Bleeding Heart Muffins

. . . . . .

My sister, Jane, was married about ten years ago. For her first baby shower luncheon, these were one of the muffins served.

1 3/4 cups all-purpose flour
2 tablespoons granulated sugar
1 tablespoon baking powder
1/2 teaspoon baking soda
1/2 teaspoon salt
2 tablespoons brown sugar, packed
1 tablespoon grated lemon zest
1/4 cup cold unsalted butter, cubed
1 egg
1 cup milk
6 tablespoons red fruit preserves, such as strawberry or red raspberry
1 teaspoon fresh lemon juice

Butter 12 muffin pan cups or line with paper baking cups.

In a medium bowl sift together flour, sugar, baking powder, baking soda and salt. Stir in brown sugar and zest until blended. Cut in butter until mixture resembles coarse crumbs. Make a well in center of mixture; set aside.

In a small bowl whisk egg and milk until blended. Add to dry ingredients. Stir just until moistened. Do not overmix.

Spoon into muffin cups.

In a small bowl combine preserves and lemon juice. Spoon 1/2 tablespoon preserves mixture onto each muffin and swirl preserves into batter using a wooden toothpick.

Bake in a 400° oven 20 to 25 minutes.

Makes 10 to 12 muffins.

Heartland Apple-Nut Muffins

. . . . . .

Healthy and delicious! These are one of my favorite muffins.

1 3/4 cups raisin-bran cereal
1 1/4 cups all-purpose flour
1/2 cup sugar
1 1/4 teaspoons baking soda
3/4 cup unsweetened apple juice
1/4 cup cooking oil
1 large egg
1/2 cup unpeeled apple, finely chopped
1/2 cup walnuts, chopped
1/2 teaspoon cinnamon

Butter 12 muffin pan cups or line with paper baking cups.
Combine first 4 ingredients in a large bowl. In a small bowl whisk together apple juice, oil and egg; add to dry ingredients and stir just until blended. Let stand 15 minutes at room temperature. Just before baking, mix apples, walnuts and cinnamon together in a small bowl and add to batter.
Spoon batter into muffin cups.
Bake in a 400° oven 20 to 25 minutes.
Makes 12 muffins.

Oatmeal Muffins

. . . . . .

Very moist and rich.

1 cup old-fashioned rolled oats
1 cup buttermilk
1/3 cup butter, softened
1/2 cup brown sugar, packed
1 egg
1 cup all-purpose flour
1 teaspoon baking powder
1/2 teaspoon baking soda
1 teaspoon salt

Butter 12 muffin pan cups or line with paper baking cups.
Soak rolled oats in buttermilk for 1 hour.
In a large bowl mix together shortening, brown sugar and egg.
In a small bowl mix together flour, baking powder, baking soda and salt; stir into butter mixture
    alternately with rolled oats and buttermilk mixture.
Fill muffin cups 2/3 full.
Bake in a 400° oven 20 to 25 minutes.
Makes 12 muffins.

Raspberry-Oat Muffins

. . . . . .

1/2 cup old-fashioned rolled oats
2 cups all-purpose flour
1/2 cup sugar
1 tablespoon baking powder
1/4 teaspoon salt
1 egg
3/4 cup milk
1/4 cup cooking oil
1/2 pint fresh raspberries

Butter 12 muffin pan cups or line with paper baking cups.
In a 10-inch skillet, over medium-low heat, toast oats until lightly browned, stirring constantly; set aside.
In a large bowl mix together flour, sugar, baking powder and salt. In a small bowl beat egg, milk and oil until blended; stir into flour mixture just until moistened (batter will be lumpy). Gently fold raspberries and toasted oats into batter.
Spoon batter into muffin cups.
Bake in a 400° oven 20 minutes.
Makes 12 muffins.

Banana-Raspberry Muffins

. . . . . .

A classy muffin.

1/2 cup all-purpose flour
1 teaspoon baking soda
1 teaspoon baking powder
1/8 teaspoon ground nutmeg
Dash of salt
1/2 cup sugar
1/3 cup oil
1 egg
2 very ripe bananas, mashed (about 1 cup)
1/2 cup fresh or frozen raspberries
2 tablespoons all-purpose flour
Sugar for sprinkling

Line 8 muffin pan cups with paper baking cups.
In a medium bowl stir together the flour, baking soda, baking powder, nutmeg and salt; set aside.
In a large bowl beat together sugar and oil; add egg and mix well. Stir in bananas.
In a small bowl toss raspberries together with 2 tablespoons flour. Add remaining flour to egg
   mixture; stir gently just until flour is moistened. Gently stir in raspberries.
Spoon into muffin cups. Sprinkle the tops of muffins very lightly with sugar.
Bake in a 350° oven 20 minutes.
Makes 8 muffins.

Banana-Nut Muffins

. . . . . .

1/2 cup butter, softened
1 cup sugar
2 large eggs
2 large very ripe bananas, mashed (about 1 cup)
2 cups all-purpose flour
1 teaspoon salt
1 teaspoon baking powder
1/2 teaspoon baking soda
1 cup buttermilk
1/2 cup pecans, chopped
1 teaspoon vanilla

Butter 12 muffin pan cups or line with paper baking cups.
In a large bowl beat together butter and sugar at medium speed until light and fluffy. Add eggs,
   1 at a time, beating well after each addition. Beat in bananas until smooth.
In a medium bowl mix together flour, salt, baking powder and baking soda.
Alternately stir, by hand, flour mixture and buttermilk into egg mixture until just moistened.
   Stir in nuts and vanilla. Do not overmix batter; it should not be completely smooth.
Spoon batter into muffin cups, filling 2/3 full.
Bake in a 400° oven 15 to 18 minutes.
Makes 12 muffins.

Soups

As I sit writing these memoirs, the
outside, accumulating in deep,
farm all those years ago with the
the electrical power always was
the kerosene heater so we all could
on and a blanket around each of us
soup and hot chocolate (from
That's when hot chocolate tasted

In winter, Mom bundled our
outside. In particular we all remem-
these from large squares of heavy
a double-thick triangle. She first

snow is falling and blowing
fluffy drifts. It reminds me of the
rough winter storms. It seemed like
going out. Dad and Mom fired up
huddle around it with our coats
to keep warm. Mom always made
"scratch") on top of the heater.
extra-special.

bodies with coats and boots to go
ber our "head shawls." Mom made
red flannel material, folded to form
tied the shawl once under our

chins and then pulled the ends to the back of our necks and tied again in a knot. In very cold weather, Dad
also wore one tied in this fashion under his hat. They kept us warm! Mom still wears her red flannel head
shawl outside around the farm. My sister, Marilyn, does a terrific re-enactment of how mom used to tie
those head shawls on us, girls and boys alike, in assembly-line fashion.

I remember being wrapped in head shawls, hats, leggings, coats, mittens and overshoes until we
practically were unable to move. Overshoes were rubber boots with metal buckles worn over our shoes.
Mom made sure we would remain warm in the cold snowy winters. We played outdoors in the snow, making
numerous snowmen of different sizes and shapes, building snow forts and lying in the snow making snow
angels. Regardless of the weather, the chores had to be done. Dad and the boys fed the farm animals, our
pet dog and the wild kittens hiding in the hay, milked the cows, gathered the eggs and broke the ice from
the top of the water troughs.

PHOTO – *Bertha Lebold Perry (youngest), my grandmother, and her parents and sister*

Cream of Broccoli Soup with Cheese

. . . . . .

On cold winter days, Cream of Broccoli Soup would stick to our bones, helping us to keep warm.

2 cups chicken broth
2 medium heads fresh broccoli, chopped, or 2 10-ounce packages frozen chopped broccoli
1 tablespoon onion, minced
1 small bay leaf
1/4 cup butter
1/4 cup all-purpose flour
Dash of pepper
2 cups milk
1 cup American cheese and/or Swiss cheese, cubed (more or less to taste)

Place chicken broth, broccoli, onion and bay leaf in a 3-quart saucepan. Bring to a boil and gently simmer, covered, about 5 minutes. Meanwhile, in a small saucepan melt butter and stir in flour and pepper; cook 1 minute, stirring constantly. Gradually add milk, stirring to make a smooth sauce. Remove from heat.

Remove bay leaf from broth and broccoli. Slowly stir sauce into broth and broccoli. Add cubed cheese. Gently heat until cheese is melted, stirring occasionally.

Serves 4 to 6.

Rosemary's Vegetable-Beef Soup

. . . . . .

A favorite of my family for years! One sleeting winter day, I let this soup simmer for hours while I was away. I arrived home to find my son Mike (then age 17) had eaten the entire potful. He said, "Mom, you always want me to eat plenty." You may want to make half this recipe, for it makes a lot. It's better warmed the second and third time.

2 pounds tenderized chuck steak, cut into bite-size pieces
12 cups tomato juice
2 to 3 cups onion, chopped
1 1/2 cups celery, chopped
Salt and pepper to taste
10 to 12 whole black peppercorns
2 tablespoons Rosemary's Soup Seasoning Mix (see recipe, page 11)
1 to 2 teaspoons garlic, minced
5 to 6 beef bouillon cubes
1 2-pound package frozen mixed vegetables
3 small potatoes, peeled and diced
1 cup cabbage, shredded *(optional)*
1/4 cup dried barley *(optional)*

In an 8-quart pan, brown the chuck steak. Add the tomato juice, onion, celery, salt, pepper, peppercorns, soup-seasoning mix, garlic and bouillon cubes. Bring to a boil and simmer slowly, uncovered, for 60 minutes.

Add frozen vegetables, potatoes, and cabbage. Return to a simmer. Simmer, covered, for 2 to 3 hours. Add barley, and simmer, covered, for 30 minutes more.

Serves 10 to 12.

Cream of Asparagus Soup

. . . . . .

I would often use fresh wild asparagus Mike picked along fencerows. It was common for my son to pick a brown grocery bag full. This soup is elegant.

1/2 cup onion, chopped
1 tablespoon butter
2 14 1/2-ounce cans chicken broth
2 1/2 pounds fresh asparagus, trimmed and cut into 1-inch pieces
1/4 teaspoon dried tarragon
1/4 cup butter
1/4 cup all-purpose flour
1/2 teaspoon salt
1/4 teaspoon pepper
3 cups half-and-half cream
1 1/2 teaspoons fresh lemon juice
Swiss cheese, shredded (*optional*)

In a large saucepan sauté onion in butter over medium heat until tender. Add broth, asparagus and tarragon. Simmer until asparagus is tender, about 8 minutes. (At this point, you can either puree the asparagus mixture, one-third at a time, in a blender or food processor, or leave asparagus in pieces.) Set aside.

In a Dutch oven, melt butter. Stir in the flour, salt and pepper. Cook and stir for 2 minutes or until golden. Gradually add half-and-half cream. Stir in the asparagus and lemon juice. Gently heat through.

Garnish with Swiss cheese, if desired.

Serves 6 to 8.

Corn and Cheddar Chowder

. . . . . .

2 tablespoons butter
2 onions, chopped
1 1/2 pounds red-skinned potatoes, unpeeled and diced
4 cups fresh or frozen whole kernel corn
4 cups half-and-half cream or milk
2 cups (or more) canned vegetable broth
3 teaspoons dried thyme or 6 teaspoons fresh thyme
4 cups medium-sharp cheddar cheese (about 12 ounces), grated
Salt and pepper to taste

Melt butter in a heavy medium saucepan over medium-high heat. Add onion and sauté until tender, about 5 minutes. Add potatoes, corn, half-and-half cream or milk, broth and thyme. Cover pan partially and simmer chowder until potatoes are tender, about 15 minutes.

Add cheese and gently stir until melted. Season to taste with salt and pepper.

Serves 4.

Corn and Potato Chowder

. . . . . .

A colorful corn chowder, as well as gooood!

2 bacon slices, chopped
1 small onion, chopped
1 potato, peeled and cut into 1/2-inch cubes
1/2 red bell pepper, chopped
2 cups (or more) milk
1 15-ounce can creamed corn
1 cup fresh or frozen whole kernel corn
1 tablespoon fresh thyme, chopped, or 1 teaspoon dried thyme
Salt and black pepper to taste
Fresh thyme, chopped

Cook bacon a in heavy large saucepan over medium heat until fat is rendered, about 3 minutes.
   Drain the fat. Add onion and cook until tender, stirring occasionally, about 8 minutes. Add potato
   and bell pepper and sauté 1 minute. Add 2 cups milk and bring to a boil. Reduce heat and simmer
   until vegetables are tender and soup thickens slightly, stirring occasionally, about 15 minutes.
Add creamed corn, whole kernel corn and 1 tablespoon chopped thyme or 1 teaspoon dried thyme to
   soup; simmer until heated through. Season to taste with salt and black pepper. Sprinkle with fresh
   thyme and serve.
Serves 4.

Tomato and Basil Soup

. . . . . .

2 cups mild onions, minced
1/4 cup butter
10 cups canned beef broth
3 pounds tomatoes, peeled, seeded and chopped (about 2 1/2 cups) and juice reserved
5 tablespoons red wine vinegar
1/4 cup sugar
1/3 cup dry white wine
Salt and pepper to taste
1/4 cup cornstarch
1 cup firmly packed fresh basil leaves, chopped

(continued on next page)

In a Dutch oven cook the onions in the butter over medium heat, stirring, until onions are softened. Add the broth, tomatoes, vinegar, sugar, wine and salt and pepper to taste. Bring the mixture to a boil; simmer, partially covered, for 25 minutes.

In a small bowl whisk together the reserved tomato juice and the cornstarch until mixture is smooth; stir the tomato juice mixture and the fresh basil into the soup. Bring the soup to a boil; reduce heat and simmer for 2 minutes more.

Serves 8 to 10.

Cream of Chicken Florentine

. . . . . .

1 2 1/2- to 3-pound chicken, cut up
6 cups water
1 10-ounce package frozen chopped spinach, thawed
1/4 cup pimiento
3 tablespoons instant chicken bouillon granules
1/4 to 1/2 teaspoon ground nutmeg
1/2 cup butter
1/2 cup all-purpose flour
3 cups milk

In a Dutch oven or large pan, combine chicken and water. Bring to a boil. Reduce heat, cover and simmer for 60 to 90 minutes or until chicken is tender and no longer pink and easily removed from the bone. Remove the chicken and let stand until cool enough to handle.

Add the spinach, pimiento, bouillon granules and nutmeg to Dutch oven. Return to boiling. Reduce heat and simmer, uncovered, for 2 minutes or until spinach is cooked. Remove from heat.

In another saucepan, melt butter. Stir in flour. Add milk all at once. Cook and stir until thickened and bubbly. Stir into spinach mixture.

Remove chicken from the bone and cut into bite-size pieces. Add to soup and heat through.

Serves 8.

Cream of Reuben Soup

. . . . . .

6 cups chicken broth
12 ounces fully cooked corned beef brisket or franks, chopped
1 8-ounce can sauerkraut, drained
1 large carrot, shredded
1/2 of a small onion, chopped
1 clove garlic, minced
1/2 teaspoon dried thyme, crushed
1/4 teaspoon pepper
1/4 teaspoon dried tarragon, crushed
1 bay leaf
3 tablespoons cornstarch
1/3 cup water
12 ounces process American cheese slices, cut up
1 cup Swiss cheese, shredded
1 cup half-and-half cream
Rye bread croutons

In a Dutch oven or large pan, combine the chicken broth, beef brisket or franks, sauerkraut, carrot, onion, garlic, thyme, pepper, tarragon and bay leaf. Bring to boiling. Reduce heat and simmer, covered, for 30 minutes.

Remove bay leaf. Stir together the cornstarch and 1/3 cup water. Stir cornstarch mixture into soup. Return to boiling. Cook the soup for 2 minutes more.

Reduce heat. Stir in the cheeses until melted. Stir in half-and-half cream. Heat through.

Serve topped with croutons.

Serves 6 to 8.

Old-fashioned Cabbage Soup

. . . . . .

1/3 cup onion, chopped
1/2 cup celery, thinly sliced
1/4 cup butter
1/2 cup all-purpose flour
8 cups chicken broth
4 cups cabbage, shredded
8 ounces or more fully cooked Polish sausage, halved lengthwise and thinly sliced
2 teaspoons snipped fresh parsley
1 to 2 teaspoons Rosemary's Soup Seasoning Mix (see recipe, page 11) *(optional)*
1/2 teaspoon pepper

In a Dutch oven cook the chopped onion and the celery in the butter until the vegetables
   are tender.
Stir flour into the vegetables until mixture is smooth. Stir in the chicken broth. Add the shredded
   cabbage; cook and stir until the soup mixture is thickened and bubbly. Reduce heat; simmer
   the soup mixture, uncovered, for 3 minutes.
Stir the sliced polish sausage, parsley, soup-seasoning mix (if desired) and pepper into the simmering
   soup mixture. Cook, uncovered, for 2 minutes more.
Serves 6 to 8.

Wild Rice Chowder

. . . . .

Very good!

2 tablespoons butter
1 onion, chopped
4 ounces smoked ham, chopped
2 celery stalks, thinly sliced
1 carrot, thinly sliced
1 1/3 cups wild rice
7 cups chicken stock or broth
1 bay leaf
1/2 cup whipping cream
Salt and pepper to taste

Melt butter in a heavy large saucepan over medium heat. Add onion, ham, celery and carrot and sauté until vegetables begin to soften, about 10 minutes. Add rice and stir to coat. Add stock or broth and bay leaf and simmer until rice is very tender, stirring occasionally, about 1 hour. Remove bay leaf. Mix in whipping cream. Season with salt and pepper.

Serves 4.

Susan's Split-Pea Soup

. . . . . .

Susan, a friend of mine, makes this yummy soup.

1 pound dried green split peas
2 quarts water
1/2 cup chicken broth
1 1/2 cups vegetable broth
1 ham bone or smoked ham hock
1 1/2 cups onion, sliced
1/2 teaspoon pepper
1/4 teaspoon garlic salt or 1/4 teaspoon minced garlic
1/4 teaspoon dried marjoram or 1 teaspoon freshly snipped marjoram
Salt to taste
1 cup celery, diced
1 cup carrots, sliced
1 teaspoon parsley flakes or 1 tablespoon fresh snipped parsley

Soak peas in 2 quarts water overnight. Drain and discard water. Combine broths with fresh water
to make 2 1/2 quarts.
Add remaining ingredients to broth mixture and simmer for 2 1/2 to 3 hours.
Serves 6 to 8.

Black Bean Soup

. . . . . .

1 tablespoon vegetable oil
1 medium onion, finely chopped
2 garlic cloves, crushed or minced
2 teaspoons chili powder
1 teaspoon ground cumin
1/4 teaspoon crushed red pepper
2 16-ounce cans black beans, rinsed and drained
1 3/4 cups chicken broth
2 cups water
1/2 cup fresh cilantro leaves, chopped and loosely packed, or 1 tablespoon dried cilantro

In a 3-quart saucepan heat oil over medium heat. Add onion and cook 5 minutes or until tender. Stir in garlic, chili powder, cumin and crushed red pepper; cook 30 seconds. Stir in beans, broth and water. Bring to boiling over high heat. Reduce heat to low and simmer, uncovered, 15 minutes. Serve soup sprinkled with cilantro.
Serves 4.

Salads

Mom made most of the clothes for the first five of us children while we were growing up. These clothes were made from feed sacks in which Dad purchased feed for the farm animals. Invariably, the sack with the prettiest pattern would be on the bottom of the pile at the feed store. Mom usually accompanied Dad to town to be sure to get the nicest looking pattern. As long as we were in diapers, both girls and boys wore little dresses made from feed sacks.

Of course, many dresses and aprons were made from the printed feed sacks. Feed sacks served a dual purpose. First was to bring feed home for the farm animals. Second was material for Mom to sew new clothes on the old treadle sewing machine. The feed sacks were made of cotton prints. Dad had to buy more than one feed sack with the same design and color in order to have enough to make a dress. When Mom's dresses and aprons and our feed sack clothes were too worn to wear anymore, they were put in our "rag bag" to be used for cleaning and dusting the house.

Mom always wore housedresses with an apron around the house, farm and garden. In those days, women did not wear slacks of any kind. Mom made her own housedresses and aprons. The dresses were colored prints and made simply, usually from one basic pattern. The aprons were the kind that went over her head, came down across her chest and tied around the waist, to help keep that housedress clean throughout the day. I remember Mom wiping her hands on her apron many times. During the summer months, a common sight of all the children, along with Mom, was bare feet. We usually went barefoot around the farm.

While I grew up, girls did not wear slacks, jeans or shorts. To keep us warm, we girls wore "leggings" in the winter under our skirts or dresses, both outside to play or to school. Leggings were made of heavy material such as wool.

PHOTO ~ *Mom and Dad, Jim, Lawrence Jr., myself and Albert*

Rosemary's Basil Potato Salad

. . . . .

New red potatoes no bigger than the end of my thumb from our local farmer's market are ideal for this salad. Larger new red potatoes can be used—just cut in bite-size pieces. I have taken this salad to many family and friend get-togethers. It's a great keeper in the refrigerator.

3 pounds small new red potatoes
1 10-ounce box frozen peas or use fresh peas in season
5 small, firm-ripe tomatoes, cut into wedges, or 20 to 25 cherry tomatoes
1/2 cup fresh basil leaves, chopped and firmly packed
1/4 cup fresh Italian parsley, chopped
1 to 2 garlic cloves, minced
1/2 to 3/4 cup green onions, chopped
1/4 cup chopped fresh chives
1/4 cup red wine vinegar
1/2 cup olive oil
Salt and pepper to taste

Scrub the potatoes well. Cut potatoes in half or into bite-size pieces and steam until just tender, about 15 minutes. Remove the steamer from the pan and let the potatoes stand at room temperature while you prepare the rest of the salad.

Put the cooled potatoes in a large bowl and add the peas, tomatoes, basil, parsley, green onions and chives.

Cut tomatoes into wedges and add to potatoes and peas.

Chop the basil and parsley and add with minced garlic cloves to potatoes and peas. Add chopped green onions, and chives.

In a small bowl whisk together vinegar and olive oil. Season to taste with salt and pepper. Toss the dressing with the salad vegetables.

Serves 8 to 10.

Leaf Lettuce Salad

. . . . . .

Mom received this recipe from a friend in San Antonio, Texas. Try this dressed-up lettuce salad instead of the usual standby. You will be asked for the recipe.

1 large head leaf lettuce, torn into bite-size pieces
1 cup celery, chopped
1 tablespoon parsley, chopped
2 green onions, chopped
1 4- to 5-ounce can mandarin oranges, drained

In a large bowl lightly toss together the lettuce, celery, parsley, onions and oranges.

Dressing:
1/2 teaspoon salt
2 tablespoons sugar
2 tablespoons vinegar
1/4 cup oil
Pepper

Blend all dressing ingredients together and add to salad just before serving.

Caramelized sliced almond topping:
1/4 to 1/2 cup almonds, sliced
2 to 3 tablespoons sugar

Place the almonds and the sugar in a heavy skillet and stir constantly over medium heat until sugar melts and turns golden and not dark. Cool almonds, break up into bite-size pieces and add to salad last.
Serves 4 to 6.

Wilted Lettuce

. . . . . .

Wilted Lettuce has been prepared for four generations of Perrys without a recipe. Mom learned by watching Grandma Perry, I learned by watching mom and my daughter, Lesly, now watches me. I will attempt to devise a recipe, which can be varied according to your taste. Being from the farm, we grew up with Wilted Lettuce, having it especially in the summer when the garden lettuce was ready. Mom would not have just one row of lettuce, she would have two or three rows, planted at about two-week intervals, and so we always had plenty. Later in the summer and fall until frost, Mom always grew endive. In those early days, as well as at our present huge family gatherings, Wilted Lettuce is a must! In order to have enough, Mom always made it in a large dishpan (about three to four gallons of lettuce). We did things up big on the farm!

2 quarts lettuce, washed, drained and torn into bite-size pieces (use garden lettuce or a mixture
   of fresh greens such as leaf lettuce, butter crunch, iceberg and endive)
1 small onion, thinly sliced (red onion is pretty mixed with the lettuce)
Salt and pepper to taste
1 to 2 teaspoons sugar (if using cider vinegar)
1/4 cup cider vinegar or red wine vinegar
3 to 4 slices bacon, chopped

In a large bowl combine lettuce and onion. Sprinkle with salt, pepper, sugar (if using cider vinegar)
   and the vinegar.
In a small skillet fry the bacon. When bacon is lightly browned and crisp, immediately pour
   over the lettuce mixture, stirring quickly to mix.
Must be served immediately.
Serves 4.

Red Raspberry Salad

. . . . . .

This salad is not only pretty, but also delicious. It tastes like fresh berries and cream. Both my Mother and I have grown red raspberries. I have made this salad many times since my younger days.

2 3-ounce packages raspberry gelatin
1 1/2 cups boiling water
2 10-ounce packages frozen red raspberries, thawed
1 8-ounce container prepared whipped topping
1 3-ounce package cream cheese, softened
20 to 30 small marshmallows

In a medium bowl dissolve the gelatin in the boiling water. Add the red raspberries. Pour into a
    9x3-inch glass dish.
Chill gelatin until set.
In a small bowl mix together the whipped topping and the cream cheese. Add the marshmallows.
    Spread mixture onto gelatin.
Wrap with plastic wrap and refrigerate until ready to serve.
Serves 8.

Fruited Chicken Salad

This summer salad, made with fresh fruit, is one of my own creations. Use it for a summer luncheon. The fruit may be varied according to personal preference and availability. Fresh nectarines could be used or plums are another in-season choice.

2 cups cooked chicken (preferably white meat), diced
2 cups fresh or canned pineapple, chopped
1 cup unpeeled apple, diced
1/2 cup oranges, diced
1 large banana, sliced
1/2 cup seedless green grapes, halved
1/2 cup toasted almonds, slivered
1/2 to 3/4 cup mayonnaise
1/4 cup pineapple juice
2 teaspoons sugar
Lettuce leaves
Fresh fruits for garnish, such as strawberries, peaches, nectarines, grapes and/or plums

In a large bowl, toss together chicken, fruits and almonds. In a small bowl mix together
    the mayonnaise, pineapple juice and sugar. Gently fold into chicken mixture.
Serve on lettuce leaves and garnish with fresh fruits.
Serves 6.

Slaw

An old family favorite.

4 to 5 cups cabbage, shredded
1/4 cup vinegar
1/4 cup water
1/2 cup sugar

Mix all ingredients together by hand, squeezing to mix well. Stir to complete mixing.
Serves 4 to 5.

Baked German Potato Salad

. . . . . .

Older brother Jim has brought this baked potato salad to our family gatherings. Now all of us have his recipe. You may want to try this delicious warm salad.

6 bacon slices, chopped
3 1/2 cups cooked new potatoes, diced
3/4 cup onion, chopped
3/4 cup green bell pepper, chopped
3/4 cup celery, chopped
1/2 cup mayonnaise
1 tablespoon prepared mustard
1 teaspoon celery seeds
Salt and pepper to taste

In a large skillet cook bacon until crisp; remove bacon from skillet reserving 2 tablespoons bacon fat.
    Crumble bacon; combine with reserved fat, potatoes, onion, green bell pepper and celery.
In a small bowl combine mayonnaise, mustard, celery seeds, salt and pepper; mix lightly. Add to
    potato mixture.
Pour into a buttered 11x7-inch baking dish.
Bake in a 400° oven for 20 minutes.
Serves 6 to 8.

Layered Basil-Vegetable-Pasta Salad

. . . . . .

Serve with thick slices of bread or dinner rolls, and this salad could be the main course.

4 cups assorted salad greens, torn into bite-size pieces
4 medium carrots, thinly sliced
1 1/2 cups pasta shells, cooked
2 cups frozen peas, thawed
1 medium red onion, diced
3/4 pound fully cooked ham, cubed
1/3 cup Swiss cheese, shredded
1/3 cup cheddar cheese, shredded

In a 3 1/2-quart bowl layer greens, carrots, pasta, peas, onion, ham and cheeses.

Make dressing:
1 cup mayonnaise
1/2 cup sour cream
2 teaspoons Dijon mustard
1/4 cup fresh basil, chopped, or 1 tablespoon dried basil
1/2 teaspoon salt
1/4 teaspoon pepper

In a small bowl combine all the dressing ingredients; spread over salad.
Cover and chill for several hours or overnight.
Serves 4 to 6.

Raspberry Delight Salad

. . . . . .

This is another favorite salad from my early years. I'm now giving it to friends. It's always a hit.

1 3-ounce package raspberry gelatin
1 cup boiling water
1 cup vanilla ice cream
3 tablespoons orange juice
1 9-ounce can crushed pineapple
1 medium banana, sliced
1/2 cup pecans, chopped

In a medium bowl dissolve gelatin in boiling water. Mix in ice cream and orange juice until blended. Chill until partially set. Add fruit and nuts. Pour into an 8x8-inch glass dish. Chill until set. Serves 6.

Strawberry Salad

. . . . . .

Tastes like fresh strawberries. Be sure to fix this salad during the winter months, and you will truly believe you have fresh berries.

2 3-ounce packages strawberry gelatin
1 1/2 cups boiling water
1 1/2 10-ounce packages frozen strawberries
1 8 1/4-ounce can crushed pineapple
1/2 cup pecans, chopped
1 cup sour cream

Dissolve gelatin in boiling water. Add strawberries and stir gently. Chill until slightly thickened. Stir in pineapple and chopped nuts. Pour half the mixture into a greased 9-inch square dish. Chill until almost firm. Fold sour cream into remaining gelatin mixture and pour over partially set gelatin. Chill until firmly set.
Serves 6 to 8.

Sauerkraut Salad

. . . . . .

Wonderful with barbecued poultry, beef and pork.

1/2 cup sugar
1-pound can sauerkraut, chopped and drained (about 2 cups)
1/2 cup celery, chopped
1/2 cup green and red bell peppers, chopped
1/2 cup carrots, shredded
1/4 cup onions, chopped

In a large bowl stir sugar into sauerkraut. Let stand 30 minutes. Add remaining ingredients.
    Cover bowl tightly and chill in refrigerator at least 12 hours before serving.
Keeps one week in refrigerator.
Serves 4.

Shrimp Salad

. . . . . .

1 1/2 pounds fresh or frozen peeled shrimp, cooked and cooled
1 medium cucumber, sliced
1 8-ounce can sliced water chestnuts
1 3-ounce can sliced ripe black olives
1 head cauliflower, cut into bite-size pieces

Toss all ingredients together in a large bowl.

Dressing:
2 cups mayonnaise
2 teaspoons dry mustard
1/4 to 1/2 cup horseradish
Dash of salt
2 teaspoons fresh lemon juice

Mix all dressing ingredients together in a medium bowl. Pour over shrimp mixture and
    toss until well coated.
Serves 4 to 6.

Sherried Cherry Salad

. . . . . .

Marilyn, my sister, picked a real taste treat with this salad.

1 cup water
1/3 cup fresh lemon juice
2 3-ounce packages black cherry or cherry gelatin
1/2 cup dry sherry or water
2 16-ounce cans dark sweet cherries, drained and syrup reserved
1/2 cup pecans, chopped
Lemon Fluff Dressing (see recipe, below)

In a small saucepan combine water and lemon juice. Bring to a boil.
In a large bowl, pour boiling mixture over gelatin; stir until dissolved. Add reserved cherry syrup
    and sherry or water; mix well. Chill until partially set. Fold in cherries and nuts. Pour into a lightly
    greased mold or 9-inch square dish.
Serve with Lemon Fluff Dressing.
Serves 6 to 8.

Lemon Fluff Dressing:
1 cup marshmallow cream
3 tablespoons fresh lemon juice
1/2 pint whipping cream

In a medium bowl beat together marshmallow cream and lemon juice. Gradually add whipping cream;
    beat until smooth and soft peaks form.

Cauliflower, Bacon and Onion Salad

......

This salad has been a Christmas tradition with my immediate family.

1 head lettuce, torn into bite-size pieces
1/2 head cauliflower, sliced
1 large red onion, sliced in rings
1/2 pound bacon, fried crisp and drained
1 cup mayonnaise
1 cup sour cream
1/3 cup grated Parmesan cheese
1 tablespoon prepared mustard

Layer some of the lettuce, cauliflower, onion rings and bacon in a large bowl. Continue layering
   over and over again until you have run out of ingredients.
In a small bowl mix together mayonnaise, sour cream, cheese and mustard. Spoon dressing over
   the top of the salad, making sure entire top of salad is covered. DO NOT MIX DRESSING
   WITH SALAD.
Cover and marinate overnight in refrigerator to allow dressing to settle down into the salad.
   Toss gently before serving.
Serves 4 to 6.

Spinach Salad

......

Use garden-fresh spinach or spinach from your local farmer's market. Look for the young small-leaf spinach.

Dressing:
1/2 cup olive oil
1/2 cup sugar
1/4 cup catsup
2 tablespoons Worcestershire sauce
1/2 cup red wine vinegar

In a medium saucepan mix together all dressing ingredients and heat until sugar dissolves. Cool.

(continued on next page)

Salad:

1 pound fresh spinach, cleaned, stems removed and torn into bite-size pieces

1 cup sliced water chestnuts

1 small purple onion, chopped

1/2 pound bacon, fried crisp and crumbled

2 to 4 hard-boiled eggs, sliced

In a large bowl mix together spinach, chestnuts and onion. Pour cooled dressing over all and toss. Garnish with bacon and eggs.

Serves 4 to 6.

Creamy Pea-Potato Salad

. . . . . .

2 pounds (about 12 to 16) tiny new potatoes

2 cups frozen peas

1/2 cup mayonnaise

1/2 cup sour cream

1 tablespoon prepared mustard

1/2 teaspoon dried tarragon, crushed

Salt to taste

1/2 cup green onions, finely chopped

1/2 cup radishes, sliced

1/2 cup Swiss cheese, shredded

Cut potatoes into bite-size pieces and steam for 15 minutes or until tender. Cool.

Steam peas for 5 to 6 minutes. Cool.

In a small bowl combine mayonnaise, sour cream, mustard, tarragon and salt.

In a large bowl combine potatoes, peas and onions. Add dressing. Toss lightly to coat mixture. Cover and chill thoroughly.

Just before serving, add radishes and mix gently. Sprinkle cheese over top.

Serves 6 to 8.

Pasta and Walnut Fruit Salad

. . . . . .

8 ounces medium pasta shells, uncooked
1 8-ounce container plain yogurt
1/4 cup frozen orange juice concentrate, thawed
1 15-ounce can mandarin oranges in juice, drained
1 cup seedless red grapes, halved
1 cup seedless green grapes, halved
1 apple, cored and chopped
1/2 cup celery, sliced
1/2 cup walnut halves

Prepare shells according to package directions; drain.
In a small bowl blend together yogurt and orange juice concentrate. In a large bowl combine shells
    with remaining ingredients. Add yogurt mixture; toss gently to coat. Cover and refrigerate until
    chilled thoroughly.
Serves 6 to 8.

Fresh Broccoli Salad

. . . . . .

Broccoli salad is a welcome addition to many Perry gatherings.

2 bunches broccoli, cut into bite-size pieces
1/2 cup green onions, chopped
1 cup pimiento, chopped
1 green or red bell pepper, chopped
1 cup Colby cheese, shredded
1/2 cup raisins *(optional)*
1/2 cup walnuts *(optional)*
1/2 cup crumbled crisp bacon *(optional)*

Wash and drain the broccoli. Cut flowerets into bite-size pieces.
Place all in medium size bowl.

(continued on next page)

Dressing:
1/2 cup sugar
1/2 teaspoon salt
1 cup mayonnaise
1 cup sour cream

Mix together all dressing ingredients and pour over salad 1/2 hour before serving.
Serves 6 to 8.

Bibb Lettuce Salad with Raspberries

. . . . . .

Impress guests with this elegant salad.

2 small heads Bibb or butterhead lettuce
1 small head leaf lettuce
1 cup fresh raspberries
1/2 cup toasted walnut halves

Dressing:
1/4 cup fresh raspberries
1 tablespoon sugar
3 tablespoons raspberry vinegar
1 tablespoon sour cream
1/2 tablespoon Dijon mustard
1/3 cup light olive oil

Tear Bibb or butterhead and leaf lettuce into bite-size pieces and place in a serving bowl.
   Top with 1 cup fresh raspberries and walnuts. Cover and refrigerate until serving time.
In a blender container combine the 1/4 cup raspberries, sugar, raspberry vinegar, sour cream
   and mustard. Blend until smooth.
With blender running, gradually add oil in a thin stream until blended. Cover and refrigerate.
   Drizzle dressing over lettuce when ready to serve.
Serves 4 to 6.

Cranberry-Walnut Relish

. . . . .

A different cranberry salad especially for the holidays.

1/4 cup brandy
1 teaspoon grated orange zest
1/4 cup orange juice
1/4 cup rice vinegar
1/4 cup red onion, minced
1/4 teaspoon mustard seeds
1/8 teaspoon salt
1/8 teaspoon freshly cracked pepper
1 cup sugar
1 12-ounce bag or 3 cups fresh cranberries
3/4 cup toasted black walnuts or walnuts, chopped

In a medium saucepan combine brandy, orange zest, orange juice, vinegar, onion, mustard seeds,
    salt and pepper. Bring to boiling over medium-high heat. Boil until liquid is reduced to 1/4 cup.
Reduce heat to medium. Stir in sugar and cranberries. Cook, stirring, until sugar dissolves.
    Continue cooking, stirring often, until most of the cranberries have popped, about 9 minutes.
Remove from heat and stir in nuts. Cool.
Cover and refrigerate until serving time.
Makes 2 1/2 cups.

Refrigerator Pickles

. . . . . .

During the summer, while cucumbers are producing in the garden, I keep a bowl of these pickles in the refrigerator. They are so convenient to serve for lunch or supper.

10 to 14 cups cucumbers, unpeeled and sliced
2 onions, sliced
1 to 2 green bell peppers, chopped
3 cups sugar
3 cups cider vinegar (5% acidity)
2 tablespoons salt
Black pepper to taste
2 teaspoons celery seeds
1 to 2 teaspoons mustard seeds
3/4 to 1 teaspoon turmeric

In a large bowl combine cucumbers, onions and peppers.
In a large saucepan bring remaining ingredients to boiling; pour boiled mixture over cucumber
  mixture. Cool. Refrigerate for one week before serving. Stir every 2 to 3 days.
Keeps in refrigerator for 3 to 4 months.
Makes about 3 1/2 quarts.

Raspberry Cream Dressing

. . . . . .

1 cup raspberries
1/4 cup raspberry vinegar
2 tablespoons sugar
1/2 cup safflower oil
1/3 cup heavy cream

Wash the berries. Press berries through a sieve set over a bowl and discard seeds.
Stir the vinegar and sugar into the berry puree.
Whisk in the oil.
Whisk in the cream just before serving.
Makes 1 3/4 cups.

Elizabeth's Salad Dressing

. . . . . .

While raising my children I had an older next-door neighbor. Elizabeth was one of those older people who took a positive, active interest in the raising of my children. Mike, Lesly and I fondly remember her. Elizabeth gave me this recipe more than twenty years ago.

1 cup sugar
1 cup catsup
3/4 cup olive oil
1 teaspoon salt
3 tablespoons vinegar
2 tablespoons onion, finely minced
2 garlic cloves, finely minced
Pepper to taste

In a large bowl whisk all ingredients together, or combine all in a blender. Refrigerate.
Makes about 2 cups.

Sweet-Sour Dressing

. . . . . .

My great aunt Jeannette Brucker Robin handed down this wonderful dressing recipe.

1/2 medium onion, finely chopped
1 cup sugar
1/2 cup white vinegar
2 teaspoons dry mustard
1 teaspoon salt
1 1/4 cups salad oil or olive oil
2 teaspoons poppy seeds

In a blender container combine first 6 dressing ingredients; blend for 3 to 5 minutes.
   Mix in poppy seeds.
Refrigerate.
Makes about 3 1/2 cups.

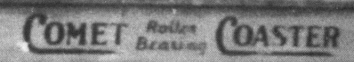

Meat & Potatoes

Meat and potatoes were the two main foods served for farm meals. Hearty meat and potato meals sustained hard-working men in the fields as well as those working in the garden and in the house. Common entrees served were fried chicken, steak, ham and pork chops, and roasted beef and pork. Gravy was made from the drippings of the fried and roasted meats and poultry. Over the years, pasta and seafood were introduced.

Dad and Mom purchased baby chicks and put them in brooder houses until they were old enough to lay eggs (the young chickens were called pullets). Then they went to the large chicken house. Pullet eggs (the first eggs laid by young chickens) were half the size of regular eggs. You have not eaten eggs until you have had a pullet egg. Mature hens would lay much larger eggs sometimes containing two yolks in each egg. Eggs were gathered in wire baskets by reaching in the nests. At times you would have to reach under the sitting hen to retrieve her eggs. Gathering eggs was the responsibility of Dad and my brothers. With so many brothers to help Dad outside, I normally helped inside. On one occasion, I was left at home and was asked to gather the eggs. When my family returned several hours later, I was still in the chicken house waiting for the hens to leave their nests. I would not reach under the hens for their eggs for fear of being pecked. That story is still being told today with much accompanying laughter. All eggs were cleaned individually by hand, and put in egg crates to be sold. Mom would clean young chickens, hardly weighing three-and-a-half pounds, and deep-fry them. The chickens did not have much meat on their bones, but were the most tender of chickens. After the pullets went to the chicken house, I used the brooder houses for my play areas. I would clean it out and play with my "treasures" there.

Chickens were caught around the leg with a hook on a long handle. Mom laid the chickens' heads on a block of wood and cut off their heads with a hatchet. The chickens were then dipped in boiling water, to loosen the feathers, after which we would remove all the pinfeathers. She then started a small fire with newspaper and ran the featherless chicken over it to remove all fine feathers. The chickens were taken to the house to clean in water and cut up, ready for the large iron frying pans, or to freeze for winter use. A few roosters were kept until they were larger, about ten to twelve pounds. The larger roosters were served instead of turkey at Thanksgiving and Christmas.

Dad also raised beef cattle and occasionally a couple of hogs. We may not have had a lot of material things while growing up, but we ate well because of living off the wealth of the land. One day my brother, Albert, said right before dinner, "Do we always have to have steak, pork chops or chicken for dinner?"

PHOTO ~ *Lawrence J. Perry, Sr.,* my father

Meat Loaf

. . . . .

Those of you who thought you did not care for meat loaf may change your mind with the following meat loaf recipe.

1 1/2 pounds ground beef
1/2 pound ground pork
2 eggs, beaten
3/4 cup onion, finely chopped
1 tablespoon Worcestershire sauce
4 strips bacon
1/2 teaspoons dry mustard
1 teaspoon salt
1/2 teaspoon pepper
1 tablespoon beef bouillon granules
1 to 2 teaspoons Rosemary's Roast Beef Seasoning (see recipe, page 10)
1 1/2 cups dry bread crumbs
3/4 cup tomato juice
Catsup

In a large bowl mix together, by hand, mix ground meats, eggs, onion, Worcestershire sauce, mustard, salt, pepper, bouillon granules, Roast Beef Seasoning, bread crumbs and tomato juice. Mold into 1 or 2 loaves, and place in a 9x13-inch baking pan.
Cover top with a layer of catsup, followed by the bacon strips (dividing for 2 loaves).
Bake in a 350° oven for 1 hour and 15 minutes. Bacon may be removed if desired before serving.
Serves 6 to 8.

Beef and Noodles

. . . . . .

Delicious, like no other beef and noodles.

3 pounds beef chuck roast, well trimmed
1 large onion, cut into chunks
8 whole cloves
1 small green bell pepper, cut into chunks with seeds and ribs removed
2 large carrots, cleaned and cut into thirds
3 ribs celery, cut into thirds
2 bay leaves
1/4 cup beef bouillon granules
2 to 3 tablespoons Rosemary's Roast Beef Seasoning (see recipe, page 10)
1/2 teaspoon black pepper
3 quarts hot water
1 cup fresh parsley sprigs
1 1-pound package medium or thin noodles

Place the meat in a large Dutch oven or heavy roasting pan with the remaining ingredients, except the noodles. Cover and bake in a 325° oven for 3 hours.

Remove the pan from the oven and transfer the meat to a chopping surface. Remove all the vegetables from the broth with a slotted spoon and discard, reserving 1 or 2 pieces of carrot. Cut meat into bite-size pieces. Chop the carrots very fine. Return the carrots and meat to the broth. Stir in the uncooked noodles. Cover the pan and return it to the oven.

Bake for 1 hour and 15 minutes more, or until the noodles are tender. Stir once during baking, being careful not to break up the noodles. Check during baking to see that the broth has not been absorbed; add additional broth as needed. Remove bay leaf before serving.

Serves 12.

Beef Stroganoff

. . . . .

I stopped using a recipe for stroganoff after making it so many times for my family. In order to write this recipe I had to make it and measure each ingredient. This is one of my daughter Lesly's favorite meals.

1 pound fresh mushrooms, cleaned and sliced
3 bunches green onions, cleaned and chopped
4 tablespoons butter
2 pounds round steak (1/4- to 1/2-inch thick)
All-purpose flour to coat meat
1 teaspoon salt
1/2 teaspoon pepper
4 beef bouillon cubes
1 1/2 cups water
1 cup sour cream
Hot cooked noodles or rice

Sauté mushrooms and onions in 2 tablespoons of the butter until browned. Set aside.
Remove fat and bone from steak. Cut into bite-size strips. In a separate skillet melt additional
   2 tablespoons butter. Toss strips of meat in flour, coating thoroughly. Brown meat in butter.
   Add salt, pepper, bouillon cubes and water. Simmer, stirring occasionally, until meat is tender,
   about 1 1/4 hours. Add mushrooms, onions and sour cream and cook until heated through.
Serve over noodles or rice.
Makes 4 to 6 servings.

Barbecue Meal in One

. . . . . .

This casserole will disappear in minutes at any gathering. Mom introduced this to our family group several years ago, and she still brings it. Men, women and children never tire of it.

1 16-ounce can lima beans
1 16-ounce can red kidney beans
1/2 pound bacon, chopped
1 pound ground beef
1 cup onion, chopped
1 16-ounce can pork and beans
1 tablespoon prepared mustard
1 tablespoon cider vinegar
1/2 cup catsup
3/4 cup brown sugar, firmly packed
1 tablespoon dried parsley or 2 tablespoons fresh parsley

Drain lima beans and red kidney beans only.

In a large skillet fry bacon until crisp; drain. Remove fat from skillet. Brown ground beef and onion in skillet.

Mix remaining ingredients with ground beef. Pour into a 3-quart casserole.

Bake in a 350° oven for 30 minutes, covered, then 30 minutes longer, uncovered.

Serves 8 to 12.

Barbecued Hamburger

. . . . . .

I didn't have a recipe for this, until I had to write one for a young fellow at the office.

2 pounds ground beef
2 tablespoons fresh lemon juice
2 tablespoons water
2 tablespoons brown sugar, firmly packed
1 teaspoon or more salt
2 teaspoons beef bouillon granules
1 cup onion, chopped
1 to 1 1/2 cups catsup
1 1/4 cups celery, chopped
1 tablespoon Worcestershire sauce
2 teaspoons cider vinegar
1 teaspoon prepared mustard
Hamburger buns

In a heavy skillet brown the ground beef lightly (no pink showing) and crumble. Drain off excess
fat. Add remaining ingredients and simmer, covered, for 30 minutes. Serve on hamburger buns.
Serves 8 to 10.

Stuffed and Rolled Flank Steak

. . . . . .

The youngest of the family, Jane, gave this yummy recipe for flank steak.

1 teaspoon salt
1/4 teaspoon paprika
1/2 teaspoon dry mustard
1/8 teaspoon ginger
2 teaspoons Worcestershire sauce
2- to 3-pound flank steak, edges trimmed

Sprinkle the seasonings on one side of the steak, then pound to tenderize.
In a large skillet sauté 2 tablespoons *chopped onion* in 1/4 cup *butter* until onion is golden.

Dressing:
1 cup bread crumbs
1/2 teaspoon salt
Pinch of paprika
2 tablespoons parsley, chopped
3 tablespoons celery, chopped
1 egg, slightly beaten

In a medium bowl combine dressing ingredients; spread dressing over steak. Roll steak loosely and
    tie in 2 places with kitchen string.
Sear rolled steak in *hot oil* on all sides in a skillet. Place steak in an oven-safe casserole.

Sauce:
3 to 4 tablespoons flour
1 cup water
2 cups dry red wine
1/4 teaspoon salt

In a small bowl combine sauce ingredients; add sauce to skillet and stir. When thickened, pour
    sauce over steak.
Bake in a 300° oven, covered, about 1 1/2 hours.
To serve, slice meat; pour a bit of sauce over all. Pass extra sauce separately.
Serves 4.

Ham Loaf

. . . . . .

Mike and Lesly's favorite meal! If you have leftovers, try slicing the loaf for sandwiches.
This Ham Loaf is served annually at a local church supper.

1 1/2 pounds smoked ham, ground
1 pound fresh lean pork, unseasoned and ground
1 cup milk
2 eggs, lightly beaten
1 cup bread crumbs
Ground cloves

In a large bowl mix together ham, pork, milk, eggs and bread crumbs. Form mixture into two
  loaves or into 10 to 12 individual loaves. Place loaves into a 9x13-inch baking pan. Sprinkle
  with ground cloves.

Sauce:
1 tablespoon mustard
1 cup brown sugar, firmly packed
1/2 cup cider vinegar
1/2 cup water
(For individual loaves, I make 1 1/2 recipe for the sauce.)

In a medium saucepan simmer sauce ingredients together for 5 to 10 minutes.
Pour sauce over loaves.
Bake in a 325° oven, uncovered, for about 2 hours. Do not cover.
After the first hour, baste loaves with sauce every 15 minutes.
Serves 6 to 8.

Glazed Ham Balls

. . . . .

Glazed ham balls are a big favorite with the men in our family. They are great for buffets and parties. They can be made a day ahead, refrigerated, then warmed.

2 pounds lean ground pork
1 1/2 pounds ground ham
3 cups soft bread crumbs
1/2 teaspoon salt
1 1/2 cups milk
1 16-ounce can pineapple chunks
1 1/2 cups dark brown sugar, firmly packed
3/4 cup cider vinegar
1 1/2 teaspoons dry mustard

In a large bowl mix together the pork and ham.

Add bread crumbs, salt and milk; mix together and shape into balls the size of walnuts. Arrange balls in a single layer in a 9x13-inch baking dish.

Bake, uncovered, in a 350° oven for 30 minutes.

While meat is baking, drain pineapple and reserve 3/4 cup juice. Cook juice, brown sugar, vinegar and mustard in a medium saucepan over medium heat and until boiling.

Spoon ham balls into two 2-quart shallow baking dishes, discarding fat. Pour juice mixture over balls in baking dish.

Bake, uncovered, 30 minutes more, stirring occasionally.

Spoon half of pineapple chunks into each baking dish and bake 15 minutes longer.

Makes 50 to 60 ham balls.

Escalloped Chicken

......

Another favorite annual church supper recipe.

3 cups boiled chicken, cubed
3 cups bread crumbs
3 eggs, lightly beaten
About 1 16-ounce can chicken broth

In a large bowl mix together chicken, bread crumbs, eggs and enough chicken broth to make
  a soupy mixture.
Put mixture into a buttered 1 1/2-quart casserole dish.
Bake in a 350° oven for 1 hour and 15 minutes.
(This recipe may be doubled. Put in a 3-quart buttered casserole dish.)
Serves 3 to 4.

Hamburger Stew

......

Kathy gave me this quick and easy "after work" meal-in-one.

2 pounds lean hamburger
1 medium onion, chopped
1 16-ounce can peas, undrained
1 16-ounce can corn, undrained
1 16-ounce can carrots, drained
1 16-ounce can green beans, drained
1 16-ounce can potatoes, drained and sliced
2 16-ounce cans tomato sauce
2 tablespoons Rosemary's Roast Beef Seasoning (see recipe, page 10)
Salt and pepper to taste

In a large skillet brown hamburger and onion together. Drain off any excess fat, if necessary.
Add the remaining ingredients.
Bring to a simmer. Simmer, covered, for 20 to 30 minutes.
Serves 8 to 10.

Chicken Pot Pie

. . . . .

A traditional Pennsylvania Dutch recipe that has now become a tradition with my family.

1 4-pound chicken, cut up
1 tablespoon butter
3 to 5 cups water
1 teaspoon salt
1/2 teaspoon dried tarragon
1/4 teaspoon saffron, crushed
1/2 teaspoon pepper

Rinse chicken. Heat butter in a 5-quart heavy saucepan. Brown chicken pieces on all sides.
  Add the water, salt, tarragon, saffron and pepper. Bring to a boil; reduce heat. Cover and simmer
  for 1 1/2 to 2 hours. Remove chicken pieces from broth to a large platter. Set aside to cool.

To the broth, add:
4 medium potatoes, peeled and cubed
2 large onions, cut into bite-size pieces
4 to 5 large carrots, cut into bite-size pieces
1 tablespoon chicken bouillon

Simmer vegetables and bouillon in broth for 10 to 15 minutes.

Flat Dumplings:
1 1/2 cups flour, unsifted
1/4 teaspoon salt
1 egg, lightly beaten
3 tablespoon milk

In a large bowl combine the flour, salt, egg and milk. Knead in the bowl to make a manageable dough.
  If mixture doesn't combine easily, add a little more milk. Turn dough out onto a kneading surface
  and knead until smooth and not sticky.
Roll dough out with a floured rolling pin to make a 12x17-inch rectangle. (It is easier to roll
  it thin if you let it stick to the surface. Loosen it, half at a time, and roll the loose half thinner;
  then repeat in another direction.) When large enough, cut into 2- to 3-inch squares and add
  to vegetable broth. Simmer gently for 15 minutes.
Remove chicken from bones, keeping in large pieces. Add to vegetables and dumplings.
Sprinkle with 1 tablespoon *parsley* and serve.
Serves 6.

Chicken and Biscuits

. . . . . .

Adults and children alike enjoy this down-on-the-farm favorite. Mom came up with a recipe after Dad had described to her what was served at a dinner prepared when neighborhood men helped a neighbor man with his harvest. My sister Kathy, since her young years, has called it "Chickie Soup."

3- to 4-pound chicken, stewed, with chicken meat removed from bones (discard skin),
    cut into bite-size pieces
6 to 8 cups reserved chicken broth for gravy
1 cup broth from stewed chicken
1/2 cup all-purpose flour
Parsley
Salt and pepper to taste
16 to 20 baked biscuits

In a large saucepan, put as much chicken broth as desired. Make a thickening with the 1 cup broth and flour. (I use a pint jar, filling jar with the 1 cup broth and adding the 1/2 cup flour. Cover jar tightly, and shake vigorously until broth and flour are well mixed with no lumps.) Before broth in saucepan starts to simmer, stir in at least 1/2 of the thickening mixture. Stir constantly over medium heat until mixture starts to simmer. If not thick enough add more thickening, stirring constantly, until mixture is of gravy consistency. Add desired amount of cut-up chicken, parsley and salt and pepper to gravy. Bring all to a slow simmer.

On individual serving plates, ladle gravy over halved biscuits. If you make your own favorite biscuits, cut into small biscuits using the middle of a metal doughnut cutter. Sprinkle additional parsley atop, if desired.

Serves 8 to 10.

Ham and Asparagus Casserole

. . . . . .

An elegant favorite for special get-togethers and for the buffet table.

1/2 cup butter
1/2 cup all-purpose flour
3 cups light cream (I use half-and-half cream)
1 1/2 cups milk
1/2 cup chicken broth
2 cups sharp cheddar cheese, grated
1/2 cup grated Parmesan cheese
Juice of one lemon
1 1/2 tablespoons onion, grated
1 tablespoon French or German mustard
1 teaspoon dried parsley
1 teaspoon salt
1/8 teaspoon pepper
1/8 teaspoon dried rosemary
1 cup sour cream
1 1/2 pounds (3 cups) fresh or frozen asparagus, cut into 1-inch pieces
3/4 pound fettuccine
2 1/4 pounds (6 cups) cooked ham, cubed or minced

In a large saucepan melt the 1/2 cup butter, then blend in flour. Slowly add the cream, milk and chicken broth. Cook until thickened, stirring constantly. Add the cheeses and the lemon juice. Add onion, mustard, parsley, salt, pepper and rosemary. Remove sauce from heat and stir in sour cream.

Clean and steam asparagus until barely tender (if using frozen asparagus, steam according to package directions.)

Break fettuccine and cook according to package directions; drain and rinse well. Mix sauce with fettuccine and ham. Layer half of the fettuccine mixture with a layer of the asparagus in a 4-quart casserole or two 2-quart casseroles, topping with a second layer of the ham-fettuccine mixture. Bake, uncovered, in a 350° oven for 30 minutes, until bubbly.

Often, I freeze one 2-quart casserole for later. Let thaw, and then bake as above for 45 minutes.

Serves 10 to 12.

Brye

· · · · · ·

Growing up on the farm, Brye was a favorite meal (often on Sunday evenings). It is actually more like pudding, but was treated as a meal (better known as "supper" on the farm) on cold winter evenings. Mom received this recipe from her German mother, Lydia Wade Brucker. Seven out of eight of us children could not wait for Mom to put ladles of this milk pudding on plates (not in bowls), so it would cool and thicken quickly. We sprinkled it with cinnamon. We always ate from around the edge of the plate where it would cool first. Of course, in those early days, mom used our own fresh milk mixed with cream from our holstein or jersey cows.

3 cups milk
1/2 cup sugar
4 tablespoons cornstarch mixed with 1/4 cup milk
Pinch of salt
Cinnamon

In a large, heavy saucepan stir milk and sugar together. Add the cornstarch-milk mixture and salt.
   Cook until the consistency of thin gravy.
Pour into shallow bowls or plates. Sprinkle with cinnamon. Serve immediately.
Serves 3 to 4.

Rigatoni with Tomato-Meat Sauce

. . . . . .

Jane says this is an excellent meat sauce for any type of pasta, but a thicker, sturdier pasta such as linguine or rigatoni can support it best.

1/4 cup olive oil
2 cups onions, chopped
2/3 cup shallots, chopped
12 garlic cloves, pressed and chopped
12 ounces veal, ground
12 ounces ground round steak
4 1/2 cups canned crushed tomatoes
2 28-ounce cans tomato puree
1 1/2 cups chicken broth
1 1/2 teaspoons dried oregano
Salt and pepper to taste
1 1/2 pounds rigatoni
1 cup fresh basil, chopped
Freshly grated Parmesan cheese

Heat oil in a heavy large saucepan over medium-high heat. Add onions, shallots and garlic; sauté until tender and golden, about 8 minutes. Add veal and round steak; sauté until cooked through, breaking up meat. Add crushed tomatoes, broth and oregano. Bring to boil. Reduce heat and simmer until slightly thickened, about 10 minutes. Season to taste with salt and pepper. (Sauce can be made one day ahead. Cover and chill.)

Cook rigatoni in a large pot of boiling salted water until just tender but still firm to bite, stirring occasionally. Drain. Transfer pasta to a large bowl.

Pour hot sauce over rigatoni. Top with the fresh basil. Pass cheese separately.

Serves 6.

Rosemary's Basil-Tomato Sauce for Pasta

. . . . . .

This sauce has a wonderful basil flavor. You may use this as a main course or as a side dish.
Great with steak or shrimp.

5 to 6 garlic cloves, thinly sliced
1/4 cup extra-virgin olive oil
4 cups fresh tomatoes (preferably Roma tomatoes), cored, peeled, seeded and chopped,
     or 1 28-ounce can crushed tomatoes
Salt and pepper to taste
1/2 cup fresh basil leaves, coarsely chopped
1/2 to 1 pound angel hair pasta or spaghetti

In a large skillet sauté garlic in oil over medium heat about 5 minutes or until garlic has cooked
     lightly and flavored the oil.
Carefully add tomatoes and salt and pepper to taste. Mix well. Bring just to boiling.
     Reduce heat. Simmer, covered, for 15 minutes, stirring occasionally.
Stir in the 1/2 cup chopped basil. Simmer covered for 15 minutes more.
While the sauce is simmering, cook angel hair pasta or spaghetti in large amount of boiling
     water until al dente. Drain thoroughly.
Top pasta with sauce.
Serves 2 to 4.

Tangy Tuna Tetrazzini

. . . . . .

1/2 pound linguine
1 teaspoon salt
1 10-ounce package frozen broccoli, chopped, cooked and drained
1 7-ounce can tuna, drained
1 10 3/4-ounce can condensed cream of celery soup
1/2 cup grated Parmesan cheese
1/2 cup water
1/2 cup slivered almonds

(continued on next page)

Add linguine and salt to 3 quarts boiling water; boil for 8 to 10 minutes, cooking until slightly underdone. Drain.

Place half of linguine in a 1 1/2-quart baking dish. Cover with chopped broccoli and half of the tuna. Spread half of the cream of celery soup and half of the Parmesan cheese atop.

Drizzle the 1/2 cup water over all.

Top with the remaining linguine, tuna and cream of celery soup. Sprinkle on remaining Parmesan cheese and the slivered almonds.

Bake in a 375° oven for 30 minutes.

Serves 4 to 6.

Shrimp Kabobs

. . . . .

Especially delicious!

1 1/2 pounds fresh or frozen jumbo shrimp in shells
1/2 cup cooking oil
1 cup Chablis or other dry white wine
1/4 cup olive oil
1 tablespoon dried oregano, crushed, or 3 tablespoons snipped fresh oregano
1/4 cup fresh lemon juice
1/4 teaspoon garlic, minced
1/4 teaspoon salt
1/8 teaspoon pepper
Fresh rosemary sprigs or 1 teaspoon dried rosemary, crushed

Thaw shrimp, if frozen. Remove shells and devein. Thread a medium-size skewer through head and tail of each shrimp to form arch. Continue until 3 or 4 skewers are packed. Place in a 13x9x2-inch baking dish.

In a medium bowl whisk together cooking oil, wine, olive oil, oregano, lemon juice, garlic, salt and pepper. Add rosemary and pour over shrimp. Cover and refrigerate 8 to 12 hours, turning occasionally.

Grill kabobs over medium-hot coals for 7 to 9 minutes or until done, turning kabobs once.

Serves 4.

Uncooked Tomato Sauce

. . . . . .

My sister, Marilyn, gave me this different and delicious tomato sauce ideally suited for our summertime tomatoes.

2 pounds fresh tomatoes
1/2 clove garlic, pressed
1/2 teaspoon salt
1/4 teaspoon pepper
1/2 cup olive oil
1/4 cup fresh basil, chopped

Peel tomatoes, core and cut in half. Squeeze halves to remove seeds. Chop tomatoes. Put tomatoes in a large bowl, adding garlic, salt, pepper and oil. Stir until combined. When mixture is thick, add the basil.
Cover and chill one hour.
Serve over hot linguine or other hot pasta.
Serves 3 to 4.

Pasta with Shrimp and Asparagus

. . . . . .

8 unpeeled jumbo fresh shrimp
4 ounces angel hair pasta
1/4 cup olive oil
2 tablespoons garlic, minced
1 teaspoon shallots, chopped
6 stalks asparagus, cut into 2-inch pieces
1/4 cup tomato, peeled, seeded and diced
1/2 cup fresh mushrooms, sliced
1/4 teaspoon salt
1/8 teaspoon crushed red pepper
1/2 cup dry white wine
1 tablespoon fresh basil, chopped
1 tablespoon fresh oregano, chopped
1 tablespoon fresh thyme, chopped
1 tablespoon fresh parsley, chopped
1/4 cup grated Parmesan cheese

Peel and devein shrimp; set aside.

Cook pasta according to package directions; drain and set aside.

Heat a 9-inch skillet over high heat 1 minute. Add oil, and heat 10 seconds. Add shrimp, garlic and shallots; cook, stirring constantly, 2 to 3 minutes or until shrimp turn pink. Add asparagus, tomato, mushrooms, salt and crushed red pepper.

Stir in wine, scraping bottom of skillet to loosen any particles, if necessary. Add pasta, basil, oregano, thyme, parsley and Parmesan cheese; toss gently.

Serve immediately.

Serves 2.

Vegetables

Across the road from the family's farmhouse in which my parents was 1942. Mom delivered my in this old house with the help of house calls in those days). In the present home was the old started their married life. The year brothers, Jim and Albert, and me our family doctor (doctors made cold blustery winter, you could see the linoleum in the kitchen rise up from the floor. In 1949 the house burned to the ground. There were four children, ages four, three, two and one at that time. My mother saved us all.

Where the old house once stood became Mom's big beautiful vegetable garden. Early each spring in April she first planted peas, green onions, radishes, cabbage and a variety of lettuces. These vegetables could withstand the cooler temperatures. The second and third weeks of May were usually warmer to plant the seeds of green beans, lima beans, carrots and sweet corn. Mom started her tomato and pepper plants in late winter on a windowsill or purchased them from the local greenhouse. Vegetables with vines, such as cucumbers, squash, melons and pumpkins, were planted near the corn so they could vine between the cornstalks. Mom tended the garden mostly by herself. At times we children would help weed. I believe Mom enjoyed having time by herself occasionally (who wouldn't with eight children?). Tending her garden was one sure way of being left alone—no one wanted to be asked to hoe. Mom had a hand-push-type cultivator with a metal wheel on the front followed by five metal curved prongs with spoon-like ends. It was held with both hands and pushed through the rows of vegetables. (No! No roto-tillers back then.)

For a quick snack during the summer, we would go to the garden, pull a carrot, pick a tomato, a pepper or one of many vegetables, clean it under the outside faucet and enjoy every bite. Today, I have my entire backyard in garden, mostly flowers, herbs, raspberries and strawberries.

PHOTO – *Rosemary Perry, myself*

Company Mashed Potatoes

The rite of passage in the Perry kitchen was when you finally mashed the potatoes with no lumps. This is a great do-ahead recipe. Prepare, cover with plastic wrap and refrigerate until ready to bake. This potato dish is particularly good with roast beef, steak or ham. Freezes well if frozen before baking.

4 cups hot seasoned potatoes, mashed (I put 1 tablespoon butter, salt and pepper to taste and milk with the potatoes when mashing)
1 cup dairy sour cream
1/3 cup green onions and tops, finely chopped
1 cup sharp cheddar cheese, grated
1/2 teaspoon seasoned salt

In a large bowl combine potatoes, sour cream, green onions and cheese. Turn into a buttered 1 1/2-quart casserole. Sprinkle with seasoned salt.
Bake in a 350° oven for 25 minutes.
Serves 6.

Note: For twice-baked potatoes, bake 3 well-scrubbed potatoes. Spoon hot potato out of shells, leaving about 1/8 inch potato lining skin, so skin will hold up when you refill them. Mash the potatoes as above. After combining all ingredients, spoon back into potato skins. Bake as directed above.
Serves 6.

Fresh Green Beans

. . . . . .

I accidentally discovered how to make these delicious green beans. I had simmered the beans for 20 to 30 minutes when I had to leave the house for awhile. I turned off the heat and left the beans on the burner, covered. When I returned an hour later, to my surprise the beans were done without overcooking.

3 slices bacon, chopped
3/4 to 1 cup onion, chopped
2 to 3 pounds fresh green beans, cleaned and broken into 1 1/2-inch pieces
Salt and pepper to taste
1 to 2 cups water

In a large heavy pan fry the bacon until almost crisp. Add the onion and continue to fry until the onions are almost transparent. Add the green beans and salt and pepper to taste. Immediately add 1 to 2 cups water.

Bring to a boil; simmer, covered, for 20 to 30 minutes. Turn off heat. Leave beans on the burner, covered, for about 1 hour. The beans will steam. Reheat slightly to serve.

Serves 6 to 8.

Creamed Peas and Potatoes

. . . . .

4 medium red potatoes, cubed
1 10-ounce package frozen peas
1 teaspoon sugar
2 tablespoons butter
2 tablespoons all-purpose flour
1/2 teaspoon salt
1/4 teaspoon white pepper
1/2 cup milk
2 tablespoons fresh dill, minced
2 tablespoons fresh parsley, minced

Steam cubed potatoes until tender.
In a small saucepan cook peas according to package directions, adding the sugar.
Meanwhile, melt butter in a medium saucepan. Add flour, salt and pepper to form a paste.
   Gradually stir in milk, stirring constantly. Simmer for 1 minute. Add dill and parsley
   and cook until thickened and bubbly.
Drain peas. Place potatoes and peas in a serving bowl.
Pour sauce over all and stir to coat. Serve immediately.
Serves 4.

Baked Cabbage

. . . . . .

1 head cabbage (about 2 1/2 pounds)
1 cup water
2 teaspoons salt
2 tablespoons all-purpose flour
2 tablespoons sugar
1/8 teaspoon pepper
3 tablespoons butter
1 cup hot milk
1 cup cheddar cheese, grated

Discard outer leaves from cabbage; wash head. Cut cabbage into 12 wedges.
Pour the water in a large skillet and bring to a boil. Add 1 teaspoon salt and the cabbage.
   Cook over medium heat, covered, for 10 minutes. Drain well.
Arrange cabbage in a buttered 12x8-inch shallow baking dish.
In a small bowl mix together the flour, sugar, remaining 1 teaspoon salt and the pepper. Sprinkle over
   cabbage. Dot with butter. Pour hot milk over cabbage. Sprinkle with cheese.
Bake in a 350° oven, uncovered, for 35 minutes.
Serves 4.

Fried Sweet Potatoes

. . . . . .

*Fried Sweet Potatoes goes back to the days of my Perry grandparents. Thanksgiving wouldn't be without them.
I have never had a "recipe". We just watched Grandma and Mom.*

4 to 5 medium sweet potatoes, boiled, peeled and sliced 1 1/2 inch thick
1/2 cup butter
1/2 cup brown sugar, firmly packed

In a medium saucepan, cover sweet potatoes with water. Bring to boil. Simmer until sweet potatoes
   are tender (soft when pierced with a knife or fork). Drain and let cool.
In a large skillet melt the 1/2 cup of butter. Roll sweet potatoes in the butter. When all sweet potatoes
   are in the skillet, sprinkle with the brown sugar. Fry at medium-low until desired crispiness.
Serves 4.

Baked Sweet Potatoes

. . . . . .

1/2 cup butter
4 to 5 medium sweet potatoes, peeled and sliced 1 1/2 inch thick
All-purpose flour
1/2 to 1 cup brown sugar, firmly packed
1/4 to 1/2 cup light corn syrup

Melt the 1/2 cup butter in a 13x9-inch shallow baking dish.
Roll sweet potatoes in flour, then in melted butter.
Place enough sweet potatoes in baking dish to fill loosely. Sprinkle with 1/2 to 1 cup brown sugar.
   Drizzle 1/4 to 1/2 cup light corn syrup over sweet potatoes.
Cover baking dish with foil.
Bake in a 350° oven for 45 to 60 minutes.
Serves 6 to 8.

Creamed Onions

. . . . . .

4 pounds small white onions
Water
1/2 cup butter
1/3 cup all-purpose flour
3/4 teaspoon salt
1 1/2 cups half-and-half cream
1/4 cup cream sherry *(optional)*

In a Dutch heat onions and 1 inch water over high heat until boiling. Reduce heat to medium-low;
   cover and cook for 10 to 15 minutes or until onions are fork-tender.
Drain onions, reserving 1/2 cup cooking liquid.
In same Dutch oven melt butter over low heat. Stir in flour and salt until blended. Gradually
   stir in reserved onion liquid, half-and-half cream and, if desired, cream sherry. Cook, stirring
   constantly, until mixture is thickened and smooth.
Return onions to Dutch oven; heat through.
Serves 6 to 8.

Broccoli Casserole

. . . . .

Lesly, my daughter, contributed this vegetable casserole (the cook that she is!). Lesly brought this good casserole to Thanksgiving dinner. Years before, it was the daughter who learned to cook. In today's world, more men are becoming good cooks. Such is the case with my son and my daughter.

1 10-ounce package frozen broccoli, chopped and thawed
1 egg, slightly beaten
1/2 cup mayonnaise
1 10 3/4-ounce can cream of mushroom soup
1 cup cheddar cheese, shredded
1 cup dried bread crumbs

In a large bowl, stir together all ingredients except the bread crumbs. Pour into a 9x9-inch buttered
   glass pan. Sprinkle top with bread crumbs.
Bake in a 350° oven for 30 minutes.
Serves 6.

Lacy French-Fried Onions

. . . . .

Oil for deep-frying
1 cup all-purpose flour
1 teaspoon baking powder
1/4 teaspoon salt
1 egg, well beaten
1 cup milk
1 tablespoon cooking oil
4 Spanish onions, sliced into 1/4-inch rings

Heat oil in deep-fat fryer to 375°.
Combine egg, milk and the 1 tablespoon cooking oil and beat well. Beat in flour, baking powder
   and salt until smooth.
Dip onion rings in batter. Gently drop into oil, a few rings at a time. Turn only once.
   Rings are done when golden brown on both sides.
Serves 4 to 6.

Sweet and Sour Beets

. . . . . .

4 to 5 strips of bacon, chopped
1 small onion, chopped
2 tablespoons all-purpose flour
3/4 cup beet juice
1/4 cups vinegar
1/3 cup sugar
Salt and pepper to taste
4 cups beets, cooked and thinly sliced

Fry bacon until crisp. Remove from skillet and drain. Add onion to bacon grease and sauté until translucent. Remove from skillet.

Add flour to grease in skillet, stirring until well blended. Add the beet juice, vinegar and sugar. Stir over medium-low heat until blended and thickened. Add salt and pepper.

Pour over beets.

Serves 4.

Cake & Ice Cream

As a teenager, I baked bread,  lots of cookies and cakes. 4-H clubs were popular for all rural children in my home area. The four Hs, with each H imprinted in a leaf of the four-leaf clover, stood for Heart, Health, Head and Hands. All eight of us children joined throughout the years.

4-H clubs met twice a month at the old Fairfield elementary school about two miles from our farm. Often we would ride our bikes to the meetings. The first year I was in 4-H I took one project: baking. We were to exhibit a loaf cake. The project booklet did not explain that a loaf cake was baked in a 9x9-inch layer pan. My cake turned out well except that it had been baked in a bread pan. I participated in 4-H for ten years, entering many county fairs and bringing home ribbons to attest to my youthful talent.

To this day I am a "from scratch" cook and baker. My own mother once told me, "It wouldn't hurt you to use a box mix once in a while." I have found it takes about the same amount of time to make cakes, cookies, etc., from a mix as it does to bake and cook with ingredients. If baking and cooking are to taste good, you must start from "scratch". Therefore, I insist on quality ingredients, no substituting. Use fresh produce and natural products. For instance, butter is the ultimate flavor in baking and cooking.

On the farm we made homemade ice cream in the wintertime. Dad or my brothers got ice from the ditch, and crushed it well enough for use in our two-gallon hand-cranked ice cream maker. Dad and the boys took turns cranking until the handle would not move. The top of the ice cream maker was covered with crushed ice, and left for a few hours to harden. Mom and I made cakes, fruit pies and chocolate sauce, and defrosted strawberries. As a special treat, our supper consisted only of ice cream, the baked sweets and the sauce and strawberries as toppings. Never were there any leftovers!

Chocolate Layer Cake

. . . . . .

I have made this rich, moist chocolate cake for thirty years. It's a must for birthdays at our house. My son Michael likes it with white frosting, and my daughter Lesly likes it with chocolate fudge icing. For other occasions, I like it with White Whipped Frosting (see recipe, page 135) topped with coconut.

2 1/2 cups sifted cake flour
1 1/2 teaspoons baking soda
3/4 teaspoon salt
3 1-ounce squares unsweetened chocolate
3/4 cup milk
5 teaspoons butter
4 eggs
2 1/4 cups sugar
1 1/2 teaspoons vanilla
1 1/2 cups dairy sour cream
Sour Cream-Chocolate Frosting or White Whipped Frosting (see recipes, page 135)

In a large bowl sift together cake flour, baking soda and salt; set aside.
Combine chocolate, milk and butter in a medium saucepan. Cook over low heat, stirring constantly, until mixture thickens. Remove from heat. Cool to room temperature.
In a large bowl beat eggs using an electric mixer at high speed until thickened. Gradually add sugar, beating until mixture is very thick and lemon-colored. Beat in vanilla.
Add dry ingredients alternately with sour cream to egg mixture, beating well after each addition.
Blend in chocolate mixture, beating at medium speed for 2 minutes.
Pour batter into 3 buttered and waxed-paper-lined 8-inch round cake pans (or two 9-inch round cake pans plus 4 to 5 paper-lined cups in muffin pan).
Bake in a 350° oven for 25 to 30 minutes or until a toothpick inserted in center comes out clean. Cool in pans for 10 minutes.
Remove from pans. Remove waxed paper; cool on racks.
Ice with Sour Cream-Chocolate Frosting or White Whipped Icing.
Serves 16.

Sour Cream-Chocolate Frosting

. . . . . .

1/3 cup butter, softened
3 cups sifted confectioner's sugar
1/2 cup dairy sour cream
2 1-ounce squares unsweetened chocolate, melted and cooled
1 teaspoon vanilla

In a medium bowl combine butter, sifted confectioner's sugar and dairy sour cream; blend well.
Add chocolate, and vanilla. Beat until smooth.
Makes about 3 cups.

White Whipped Frosting

. . . . . .

I found this frosting recipe at a 4-H meeting when I was about fifteen. I use this frosting for many different cakes. It's long been a favorite.

1 cup milk
1/2 cup all-purpose flour
1 cup sugar
1/2 cup butter
1/2 cup shortening
1 teaspoon vanilla

In a medium saucepan whisk together milk and flour. Cook over medium-low heat, stirring
    constantly, until mixture is thickened. Remove from heat and let stand until cooled.
In a medium bowl beat sugar, butter and shortening together until light and fluffy. Add vanilla.
Add the cooled, thickened milk mixture and continue to beat until mixture looks like whipped cream.
(Can be made a day ahead.)
Makes about 3 cups.

Zucchini-Chocolate Cake

. . . . .

Summer gardens bring lots of zucchini. A way to use it without anyone being able to "see" it is in this moist cake. No icing is needed. Great for picnics and reunions.

2 1/2 cups sifted all-purpose flour
1/4 cup baking cocoa
1 teaspoon baking soda
1 teaspoon salt
1/2 cup butter, softened
1/2 cup cooking oil
1 3/4 cups sugar
2 eggs
1 teaspoon vanilla
1/2 cup buttermilk
2 cups zucchini, unpeeled and grated (I use a food processor)
1 6-ounce package or 1 cup semisweet chocolate pieces
3/4 cup walnuts, chopped
Walnut halves

In a medium bowl sift together flour, cocoa, baking soda and salt; set aside.
In a large bowl, using an electric mixer at medium speed, cream together butter, oil and sugar until
   light and fluffy. Beat in eggs, one at a time, beating well after each addition. Blend in vanilla.
Add dry ingredients alternately with buttermilk to creamed mixture, beating well after each addition.
Stir in zucchini. Pour batter into a buttered 13x9-inch baking pan. Sprinkle with chocolate pieces
   and walnuts.
Bake in a 325° oven for 55 minutes or until a toothpick inserted near center comes out clean.
   Cool in pan on a wire rack. Cut into squares.
Serves 12 to 16.

Hickory Nut Cake

. . . . . .

Believe it or not, I enjoy gathering hickory nuts each year (you cannot buy them). You must remove the outer hulls, let them dry for a couple of months and then crack and pick out the nutmeats. For 1/4 cup of nutmeats, it takes about an hour of picking. To me it is well worth the effort. They have a unique flavor that cannot be substituted. They are not only delicious in cakes, but also in cookies, candies and breads.

1/2 cup butter, softened
1 1/4 cups sugar
2 eggs
2 cups plus 2 tablespoons sifted cake flour
2 teaspoons baking powder
1/2 teaspoon salt
3/4 cup milk
1 cup hickory nuts, coarsely chopped
1 teaspoon vanilla

In a large bowl, using an electric mixer on medium speed, cream butter; add sugar gradually and beat until fluffy. Blend in eggs, one at a time, beating after each addition until light and fluffy.

In a medium bowl mix together flour, baking powder and salt. Stir into creamed mixture alternately with the milk. Add the nuts with the last addition of flour. Blend in vanilla.

Pour batter into 2 buttered and waxed-paper-lined 8-inch round cake layer pans, or in a 13x9-inch buttered baking pan.

Bake in a 350° oven for 25 to 30 minutes, or until a toothpick inserted in center comes out clean.

Frost with White Whipped Frosting (see recipe, page 135).

Serves 12 to 16.

Rosemary's Sunshine Cake

. . . . . .

A refreshing, delicious-tasting cake. This cake is good anytime, but serve at Easter for a springtime treat.

2 1/2 cups sifted cake flour
1 2/3 cups sugar
3 1/2 teaspoons baking powder
1 teaspoon salt
3/4 cup milk
2/3 cup shortening
3 eggs
1/2 cup milk
1 teaspoon vanilla
Pineapple Filling (see recipe, page 139)
White Whipped Frosting (see recipe, page 135)
Shredded coconut *(optional)*

In a large bowl combine flour, sugar, baking powder and salt.
Add the 3/4 cup milk and the shortening, beating with an electric mixer at medium speed for
   2 minutes.
Add eggs, the 1/2 cup milk and the vanilla. Beat 2 minutes more.
Pour batter into 2 buttered and waxed-paper-lined 9-inch round cake layer pans.
Bake in a 350° oven for 30 to 35 minutes or until a toothpick inserted near center comes
   out almost clean.
Let cool in pans for 10 minutes. Invert one layer on a cake plate, and the other layer on wire rack.
Let cool.
To assemble, spread Pineapple Filling between the two layers of cake.
Frost with White Whipped Frosting.
If desired, sprinkle shreds of coconut all around the sides and top of cake.
Serves 16.

Pineapple Filling

. . . . . .

1/2 cup sugar
3 tablespoons cornstarch
1/2 teaspoon salt
3/4 cup pineapple juice
1 cup crushed pineapple, well drained
1 tablespoon butter
1 teaspoon fresh lemon juice
Shredded coconut *(optional)*

In a large saucepan mix together sugar, cornstarch and salt. Gradually stir in pineapple juice.
   Bring to boiling over medium heat, stirring constantly. Boil 1 minute. Remove from heat.
Stir in pineapple, butter and lemon juice. Cool thoroughly.
Use with Rosemary's Sunshine Cake (see recipe, page 138).

Banana Spice Cake

. . . . . .

Grandma Bertha Perry handed down this cake, and it is just as good today as it was in her era.

2 1/2 cups sifted cake flour
2 1/2 teaspoons baking powder
1/2 teaspoon soda
3/4 teaspoon salt
1/8 teaspoon cloves
1 1/4 teaspoons cinnamon
1/2 teaspoon nutmeg
1/2 cup butter, softened
1 1/4 cups sugar
2 eggs
1 teaspoon vanilla
4 to 5 ripe bananas, mashed (about 1 1/2 cups)

In a medium bowl combine flour, baking powder, soda, salt and spices. Set aside.

In a large bowl cream butter, using an electric mixer at medium speed. Add sugar gradually and continue beating until light and fluffy.

Add eggs, one at a time, beating after each addition until fluffy. Stir in vanilla.

Add flour mixture alternately with bananas, a small amount at a time, mixing after each addition until smooth.

Pour batter into a buttered 13x9-inch baking pan.

Bake in a 350° oven for 30 to 35 minutes or until a toothpick inserted near center comes out almost clean.

Top with White Whipped Frosting (see recipe, page 135).

Serves 12 to 16.

Banana-Nut Cake

. . . . . .

I cannot remember where this recipe came from, but Mom and I made it while I was growing up.
I still make it and it disappears as quickly today as it did forty years ago.

2 1/2 cups sifted cake flour
1 1/4 teaspoons baking powder
1 2/3 cups sugar
1 1/4 teaspoons baking soda
1 teaspoon salt
1/3 cup butter
1/3 cup shortening
2/3 cup buttermilk
3 ripe bananas, mashed (about 1 1/4 cups)
2 large eggs
2/3 cup nuts, chopped
Cream Cheese Frosting (see recipe, page 142)

In a large bowl mix together cake flour, baking powder, sugar, baking soda and salt.
Add butter, shortening, 1/3 cup buttermilk and bananas. Beat with an electric mixer at medium
    speed for 2 minutes.
Add remaining buttermilk and eggs. Beat for 2 minutes more. Fold in nuts.
Pour batter into a buttered 13x9-inch baking pan.
Bake in a 350° oven for 35 to 40 minutes or until a toothpick inserted near center comes
    out almost clean.
Spread with Cream Cheese Frosting.
Serves 12 to 16.

Cream Cheese Frosting

. . . . . .

1 8-ounce package cream cheese, softened
3/4 stick (6 tablespoons) butter, softened
2 teaspoons vanilla
1 16-ounce package confectioner's sugar
1/2 cup black walnuts or English walnuts, chopped (*optional*)

In a large bowl combine cream cheese, butter and vanilla. Beat with an electric mixer at medium
    speed until light and fluffy. Gradually add confectioner's sugar until well mixed. If desired,
    stir in walnuts.
Spread frosting on top of cooled cake.
Keep refrigerated.
Makes about 3 cups.

Carrot Cake

. . . . . .

2 cups sugar
1 1/2 cups vegetable oil
4 eggs
2 cups all-purpose flour
1 teaspoon salt
1 teaspoon baking soda
2 teaspoons cinnamon
3 cups raw carrots, grated
1/2 cup black walnuts or English walnuts, chopped (*optional*)
1 tablespoon vanilla

In a large bowl, using an electric mixer at medium speed, beat sugar, vegetable oil and eggs together
    until light and fluffy.
In a small bowl combine flour, salt, baking soda and cinnamon; add to egg mixture, mixing well.
    Add carrots, walnuts (if desired) and vanilla; mix well.
Pour into a well-buttered 13x9-inch pan.
Bake in a 325° oven for 45 to 50 minutes or until a toothpick inserted in center comes out almost clean.
Frost with Cream Cheese Frosting (see recipe, above).
Serves 12 to 16.

Maraschino Cherry Cake

......

A special cake for your mother's birthday! As a teenager I would make this pretty cake for my mother.

2 1/4 cups sifted cake flour
1 1/3 cups sugar
3 teaspoons baking powder
1 teaspoon salt
1/2 cup soft shortening
1/4 cup maraschino cherry juice
16 maraschino cherries, cut into eighths
1/2 cup milk
4 egg whites (1/2 to 2/3 cup), unbeaten
1/2 cup pecans, chopped

In a large bowl mix together flour, sugar, baking powder and salt.
Add shortening, cherry juice, cherries and milk. Beat for 2 minutes using an electric mixer
  on medium speed. Add egg whites. Beat 2 minutes more. Fold in nuts.
Pour batter into 2 buttered and waxed-paper-lined 8-inch round cake layer pans, or into
  a 13x9-inch buttered baking pan.
Bake in a 350° oven for 30 to 35 minutes or until a toothpick inserted near center comes
  out almost clean.
Frost with White Whipped Frosting (see recipe, page 135).
Serves 12 to 16.

Raspberry Angel Food Cake

. . . . . .

I grow my own raspberries, so there are plenty to make this good cake. Red raspberries are my favorite for this cake.

10 to 12 egg whites (about 1 1/2 cups)
1 1/4 teaspoons cream of tartar
1 teaspoon vanilla extract
1/2 teaspoon almond extract
1/2 cup sugar
1 cup cake flour
2 cups fresh raspberries

In a large bowl, using an electric mixer at medium speed, beat egg whites until frothy; then beat in cream of tartar until soft peaks form. Add the extracts. Gradually beat in sugar until stiff, scraping sides of bowl occasionally. Gradually sift flour over beaten whites, in about 4 increments, gently folding into batter. Add raspberries with last addition of flour.
Pour into an ungreased 10-inch tube pan.
Bake in a 325° oven for 35 to 40 minutes or until lightly browned and entire top appears dry.
Immediately invert cake pan; cool completely, about 1 hour. Remove from tube pan.
Frost with Mary Jane's Frosting (see recipe, below).
Serves 16.

Mary Jane's Frosting

. . . . . .

My mother Mary Jane used this frosting many times during World War II when sugar was rationed.

3/4 cup white corn syrup
2 egg whites, beaten to soft peeks
1/2 teaspoon vanilla

In a medium saucepan heat corn syrup to boiling; pour over beaten egg whites, beating with an electric mixer on medium speed while pouring.
Beat until cool and spreadable. Add vanilla; mix well.
Makes about 4 cups.

Peanut Butter Broiled Icing

. . . . . .

Growing up, my brothers and sisters called this icing "Burnt Icing." It was one of our favorites atop chocolate cake. The cake must be in a flat pan, not a layer cake. We would watch the cake under the broiler while the icing was bubbling. The icing would tend to get somewhat brown; thus, to this day we call it "Burnt Icing."

2/3 cup brown sugar, firmly packed
4 tablespoons butter, softened
4 tablespoons half-and-half cream or canned evaporated milk
4 tablespoons peanut butter
1/2 cup peanuts, chopped *(optional)*

Mix all ingredients together in a medium bowl. Spread on top of cooled cake in pan.
   Put cake under broiler until icing bubbles all over. Watch diligently; DO NOT BURN.
Makes about 1 cup.

Vanilla Ice Cream

. . . . . .

6 eggs, beaten
3 cups sugar
5 tablespoons cornstarch
4 cups milk
Pinch of salt
2 handfuls small marshmallows
4 cups half-and-half cream
3 tablespoons vanilla

In a Dutch oven bring to boil the eggs, sugar, cornstarch, milk, salt and marshmallows.
   Simmer for 1 minute. Cool—can be refrigerated overnight. Stir in the half-and-half cream
   and vanilla.
Pour into an ice cream freezer. Freeze according to manufacturer's directions.
Makes 1 gallon.

Peach Ice Cream

. . . . .

An old-time peach ice cream that tastes like a peach orchard in a bowl.

5 egg yolks
1 1/2 cups sugar
4 cups whipping cream or half-and-half cream
4 cups washed fresh ripe peaches, peeled and sliced
2 cups milk
1 tablespoon vanilla

In a heavy medium saucepan combine the egg yolks, 1 1/4 cups of the sugar and 3 cups of the whipping cream or half-and-half cream. Cook and stir over medium heat, cooking mixture until it just comes to a boil. Remove from heat.
Stir in remaining whipping cream or half-and-half cream. Chill.
Meanwhile, in a blender or food processor, process the peach slices until they're almost pureed. Add remaining 1/4 cup sugar. Stir until mixed.
Combine the egg mixture with the blended peaches, milk and vanilla.
Freeze in a 3- to 4-quart ice cream freezer according to manufacturer's directions.
Makes 3 quarts.

Old-fashioned Raspberry Ice Cream

. . . . .

4 cups raspberries
3/4 cup sugar
1/8 teaspoon salt
1 cup heavy or whipping cream
1 cup milk

In a food processor with a knife blade attached, blend raspberries until pureed. Press raspberries through a medium-mesh sieve into a large bowl (about 1 1/2 cups puree) and discard seeds.
With a wire whisk, beat sugar and salt into raspberry puree until sugar is dissolved. Add cream and milk and whisk until blended. Cover and refrigerate until well chilled, about 1 hour.
Pour chilled mixture into an ice cream can or freezer chamber of ice cream maker. Freeze according to manufacturer's directions.
Makes about 1 quart.

Homemade Frozen Custard

. . . . . .

4 cups milk
4 eggs
1 1/4 cups sugar
1/3 cup cornstarch
1/8 teaspoon salt
1 14-ounce can sweetened condensed milk
2 tablespoons vanilla

In a large heavy saucepan, bring milk to a boil.
Meanwhile, in a large bowl beat eggs. Add sugar, cornstarch and salt. Mix well. Gradually add
  a small amount of hot milk to egg mixture and return all to the saucepan. Cook and stir
  constantly for 6 to 8 minutes or until mixture thickens and coats a spoon.
Gradually stir in condensed milk and vanilla. Mix well. Chill for 3 to 4 hours.
Pour into an ice cream freezer. Freeze according to manufacturer's directions.
Makes 1 1/2 quarts.

Favorite Vanilla Ice Cream

. . . . . .

4 eggs
2 1/2 cups sugar
3 cans evaporated milk
4 cups milk
4 1/2 teaspoons vanilla
1/2 teaspoon salt

In a large bowl beat eggs and sugar until thick. Add the evaporated milk and beat well.
  Mix in milk, vanilla and salt.
Pour into an ice cream freezer.
Freeze according to manufacturer's directions.
Makes 1 gallon.

Cheesecakes

One of the duties at mealtime was setting the table. One of us girls had the pleasure of this responsibility. My sister, Jane, said setting the table for company, special events or at holidays was a special treat. At these special times we could use special table settings and linens. Jane remembers deciding with Mom which china to use and which glassware looked best. There was always a special tablecloth or a special dish with its own history and story. Setting the table became a glimpse into the past. It also impressed Jane that when you put a lot of effort into the making of food, it is important to serve it in a lovely setting. I remember we called the sugar, salt, pepper, butter and jelly/jam the "vittles," for they were always put on the table for any meal.

When unexpected company arrived, Mom always invited them to stay for supper, saying, "We don't have much, but what we've got is awful good."

At the end of each meal dishes had to be washed, dried and put away by hand. The dishwashers were us eight children. My first memories of washing dishes are of me standing on a stool or a chair turned backward against the kitchen cabinets. Our kitchen countertop was long, and after meals it would be fully stacked with dishes to wash. To dry dishes, I sat on the opposite countertop, wiping dishes with white cotton feed sackcloths Mom had hemmed. The boys usually did not have to help with the dishes, but since I was the only girl until I was seven, they pitched in sometimes.

PHOTO ~ *Lawrence and Mary Jane Perry,* my parents

Lime Cheesecake

. . . . . .

I never cease to win compliments when serving this cheesecake. Lime cheesecake is the Perry family's favorite. It is a velvety-smooth, refreshing cheesecake. If you prefer lemon, just substitute it for the lime.

Crust:
1 1/2 cups vanilla cookie wafer crumbs
1/3 cup butter, melted
1/4 teaspoon cinnamon

In a medium bowl mix the cookie crumbs, melted butter and cinnamon together with a fork.
Press mixture onto the bottom and 1 1/2 inches up sides of a 9-inch springform pan. Set aside.

Filling:
2 8-ounce packages cream cheese, softened
4 large eggs
1 16-ounce container sour cream
1 1/4 cups sugar
1 teaspoon vanilla extract
1/2 teaspoon salt
1/3 cup fresh lime juice (approximately 3 limes)
1 tablespoon lime peel, grated
Lime slices for garnish

In a large bowl, using with an electric mixer at medium speed, beat cream cheese and eggs together until smooth. With mixer at low speed, beat in sour cream, sugar, vanilla extract, salt, lime juice and lime peel until well blended.
Pour filling into vanilla cookie wafer crust.
Bake in a 350° oven for 50 minutes (center of cheesecake may appear loose).
Cool cheesecake in pan on a wire rack.
Refrigerate cheesecake at least 6 hours or until well chilled.
To serve, carefully remove side of pan. Garnish with lime slices.
Serves 16.

Frangelico Cheesecake

. . . . . .

Crust:
1 1/2 cups vanilla cookie wafer crumbs
1/3 cup butter, melted
3 tablespoons sugar

In a medium bowl mix the cookie crumbs, melted butter and sugar together with a fork.
Press mixture onto bottom and slightly up sides of a 9-inch springform pan.

Filling:
3 8-ounce packages cream cheese, softened
1/2 cup sugar
1/3 cup maple syrup, at room temperature
1/2 teaspoon salt
3 large eggs, at room temperature
1/4 cup Frangelico (hazelnut liqueur)
1 tablespoon fresh lemon juice
1 teaspoon vanilla extract
2 1/2 cups sour cream, at room temperature

In a large bowl, using an electric mixer at medium speed, beat the cream cheese until fluffy, gradually
    adding the sugar, maple syrup and salt. Beat in the eggs, one at a time, followed by the Frangelico,
    lemon juice and vanilla. Blend in the sour cream.
Pour the filling into the cookie wafer crust.
Bake in a 350° oven for 55 minutes.
Let the cheesecake cool thoroughly on a wire rack.
Cover cheesecake with plastic wrap and chill overnight or for at least 6 hours.
To serve, carefully remove side of pan.
Serves 16.

Irish Cream Cheesecake

. . . . . .

It's marvelous! I have made quite a hit with this cheesecake during the holiday season. It's flavored with Irish cream liqueur.

Crust:

1 1/2 cups chocolate sandwich cookie crumbs
1/3 cup butter, melted
2 tablespoons sugar

In a medium bowl mix cookie crumbs, melted butter and sugar together with a fork. Press mixture onto the bottom of a 9-inch springform pan. Bake crust in a 350° oven for 8 minutes. Let cool on a wire rack.

Filling:

3 8-ounce packages cream cheese, softened
7 tablespoons sugar
1 tablespoon all-purpose flour
2 large eggs
1/4 cup plus 2 tablespoons sour cream, at room temperature
1/4 cup plus 2 tablespoons Irish cream liqueur
1 teaspoon vanilla extract

Using an electric mixer at medium speed, beat cream cheese and sugar together in a large bowl until smooth. Beat in flour. Add eggs, one at a time, beating just until combined. Mix in remaining ingredients.

Pour filling into crust.

Bake in a 350° oven for 10 minutes. Reduce oven temperature to 250° and bake for 40 minutes more.

Cool cake in pan on a wire rack. Chill overnight.

To serve, carefully remove side of pan.

Serves 16.

Coconut Cream Cheesecake

. . . . . .

A creamy coconut taste treat.

Crust:
1 1/2 cups vanilla cookie wafer crumbs
1/3 cup butter, melted
3 tablespoons sugar

In a medium bowl mix the cookie crumbs, melted butter and sugar together with a fork.
   Press mixture onto bottom and slightly up sides of a 9-inch springform pan.
Bake in a 350° oven for 7 to 8 minutes. Set aside.

Filling:
3 8-ounce packages cream cheese, softened
1 1/2 cups sugar
4 eggs, at room temperature
2 egg yolks, at room temperature
2 cups flaked coconut
1 cup whipping cream
1 teaspoon fresh lemon juice
1/2 teaspoon vanilla
1/2 teaspoon almond extract
Toasted coconut *(optional)*

In a large bowl, using an electric mixer at medium speed, beat cream cheese and sugar until smooth.
   Beat in eggs and yolks, one at a time. Mix in flaked coconut, whipping cream, fresh lemon juice,
   vanilla and almond extract.
Pour filling into crust.
Bake in a 300° oven until edges of filling are firm, about 70 minutes.
Let cool completely. Remove from pan.
Cover cheesecake with plastic wrap and refrigerate at least 4 hours before serving.
If desired, sprinkle with toasted coconut.
Serves 16.

White Chocolate Cheesecake

. . . . . .

The raspberry sauce not only makes this cheesecake delicious, but attractive. I enjoy taking this cheesecake to family and friend gatherings. Not one piece ever returns home with me. One of my personal favorites!

Crust:
2 cups vanilla cookie wafer crumbs
1/2 cup butter, melted
1/4 cup sugar

In a medium bowl mix the cookie crumbs, melted butter and sugar together with a fork.
Press onto the bottom and up 1 inch on sides of a 9-inch springform pan.

Filling:
4 8-ounce packages cream cheese, at room temperature
1 cup sugar
3/4 cup white chocolate, grated
3 tablespoons crème de cassis liqueur or framboise *(optional)*
4 large eggs, at room temperature
2 cups dairy sour cream, at room temperature
1/4 cup sugar
1 teaspoon vanilla extract

In a large bowl, using an electric mixer at medium speed, beat the cream cheese until smooth.
    Gradually beat in the 1 cup of sugar, grated chocolate and, if desired, crème de cassis or framboise,
    beating just until well blended. Beat in eggs, one at a time, and continue beating until smooth.
Pour filling into crust. Tap pan lightly two to three times to remove bubbles.
Place oven rack one-third of the way up from bottom of oven.
Bake in a 350° oven for 40 to 45 minutes. Edges may crack, but center will not appear set.
Cool 10 minutes on a wire rack.
In a small bowl combine sour cream, 1/4 cup sugar and vanilla extract. Stir with spoon until blended.
    Pour over top of the slightly cooled cake. Spread evenly to edges. Return to oven for 10 minutes
    more. Topping will quiver, but appear set.
Cool completely.
Refrigerate at least 12 hours.

Raspberry Sauce:
1 cup raspberries
1 tablespoon cornstarch
1 tablespoon light corn syrup

(continued on next page)

Before serving cheesecake, in a small saucepan combine raspberries and just enough cornstarch and
    corn syrup to sweeten and thicken when cooked.
Cook down until thickened. Cool to room temperature.
To serve, carefully remove side of pan.
Top cake with sauce before serving.
Serves 16.

Chocolate-Amaretto Cheesecake or
Chocolate-Crème De Menthe Cheesecake

. . . . . .

My sister, Marilyn, provided a lower fat cheesecake that is absolutely delicious. By substituting crème de menthe for the amaretto, you will have a wonderful Chocolate-Crème de Menthe Cheesecake. A wonderful holiday addition.

6 chocolate cookie wafers, finely crushed
1 1/2 cups light process cream cheese
1 cup sugar
1 cup low-fat cottage cheese
1/4 cup plus 2 tablespoons unsweetened cocoa
1/4 cup all-purpose flour
1/4 cup amaretto or crème de menthe
1 teaspoon vanilla
1/4 teaspoon salt
1 egg
2 tablespoons semisweet chocolate mini morsels

Sprinkle chocolate cookie wafer crumbs in bottom of a 7- or 8-inch springform pan. Set aside.
In a food processor bowl with a knife blade attached, add cream cheese, sugar, cottage cheese,
    unsweetened cocoa, flour, amaretto or crème de menthe, vanilla and salt, processing until smooth.
    Add egg and process just until blended. Fold in chocolate morsels.
Slowly pour mixture over crumbs in pan.
Bake in a 300° oven for 65 to 70 minutes for a 7-inch pan or 45 to 50 minutes for an 8-inch pan.
Let cool in pan on a wire rack.
Cover cheesecake and chill at least 8 hours.
Remove side of pan and transfer cheesecake to a serving platter.
Serves 12.

Creamy Chocolate Lace Cheesecake

. . . . .

Sinfully delicious!

Crust:
1 1/2 cups (about 24 wafers) chocolate cookie wafer crumbs
1/2 cup almonds, finely chopped
1/4 cup butter, melted

In a large bowl combine crust ingredients and mix well.
Press crust onto bottom and up sides of a buttered 9-inch springform pan.
Refrigerate while preparing filling.

Filling:
2 8-ounce packages cream cheese, softened
2/3 cup sugar
3 eggs
1 12-ounce package or 2 cups semisweet chocolate chips, melted and cooled
1 cup whipping cream
2 tablespoons butter, melted
1 teaspoon vanilla

In a large bowl, using an electric mixer, beat cream cheese and 2/3 cup sugar at medium speed until
  smooth and creamy. At low speed, add eggs, 1 at a time, beating just until blended. Add melted
  chocolate chips and beat well. Add whipping cream, the 2 tablespoons butter and 1 teaspoon
  vanilla. Beat until smooth.
Pour filling into crust-lined pan.
Bake in a 325° oven for 55 to 65 minutes or until edges are set. Center of cheesecake will be soft.
Cool in pan 5 minutes. Carefully remove sides of pan. Cool completely.

Topping:
1 cup dairy sour cream
1 1/2 teaspoons vanilla
1 teaspoon sugar
1/2 ounce unsweetened chocolate, melted

In a small bowl combine sour cream, vanilla and sugar; stir until smooth.
Spread topping over cooled cheesecake.
Drizzle with the 1/2 ounce melted chocolate in a lace pattern.
Refrigerate several hours or overnight before serving.
To serve, carefully remove side of pan.
Serves 16.

Pumpkin Cheesecake

. . . . .

Crust:

2 cups vanilla wafer cookie crumbs

3/4 cup pecans, ground

6 tablespoons unsalted butter, melted

2 tablespoons golden brown sugar, firmly packed

Combine all ingredients in a medium bowl and stir until moist clumps form. Press mixture
   onto bottom and 1 inch up sides of a 10-inch springform pan.

Bake crust in a 425° oven for 7 to 10 minutes.

Cool on a wire rack.

Filling:

4 8-ounce packages cream cheese, softened

1 1/2 cups brown sugar, firmly packed

5 large eggs

2 large egg yolks

1 16-ounce can solid-pack pumpkin

1/4 cup all-purpose flour

1/4 cup brandy *(optional)*

1 1/4 teaspoons allspice

1 1/4 teaspoons cinnamon

In a large bowl, using an electric mixer at medium speed, beat cream cheese just until smooth.
   Gradually beat in brown sugar. With mixer at low speed, beat in eggs, egg yolks, pumpkin, flour,
   brandy (if desired), allspice and cinnamon just until blended, occasionally scraping sides of bowl
   with a rubber spatula.

Pour filling into crust in pan.

Bake in a 425° oven for 15 minutes. Reduce heat to 275° and bake 1 hour more.

Topping:

In a small bowl combine 2 cups *sour cream* and 2 teaspoons *granulated sugar.*

Remove cheesecake from oven. Spread sour cream mixture evenly on top of cheesecake.

Bake 5 to 10 minutes more until sour cream topping is set.

Cool cheesecake in pan on a wire rack.

Refrigerate cheesecake 4 hours or until well chilled.

To serve, carefully remove side of pan.

Serves 16.

Pies

Wild black raspberries and blackberries were picked every year in the woods and at the steep edges of the ditches. The largest berries came from the edges of the ditch where the plants received protection and plenty of moisture. During our growing years, Jim and Mick were the berry pickers. We would get up in the morning to find them already gone with their pails to pick berries. Many times we would pick up Grandma Perry and go to her woods to pick berries together.

Strawberries, raspberries and gooseberries either were raised in our garden or found growing wild on our farm. I was in my early teens when blueberry farms first started. It was customary for the Perry bunch to arrive with their pails at the blueberry patch before the dew on the leaves and berries had a chance to dry.

The tiny wild strawberry has a heady, intense flavor. We found patches of the wild ones along river and creek banks, along railroad tracks and in woods. We had to be patient. It took much longer to fill our pail with the wild, delicate berries that were no larger than the end of our smallest finger. Mike picked wild strawberries in woods and along railroad tracks. He knew his mother would make him jam with those most flavorful of all strawberries.

Annual journeys to Michigan were made by Mom and Dad and the older children to pick quarts of sour and sweet cherries, and bushels of peaches, plums and pears. In the fall months, bushels of many different varieties of apples were picked at area orchards.

While the fresh fruits and berries were plentiful, Mom made many pies, cobblers, shortcakes and jams. She would divide berries or sliced peaches into small individual bowls and serve with sugar and with our own rich whole milk poured on top. Breakfast bowls of cereal were covered liberally with fresh fruit. One of our favorite ways to eat berries was as we picked them. It's a wonder that any berries made it to our pails.

In later years Mom grew her own red raspberries and purple raspberries. Purple raspberries are a combination of black and red raspberries. The berries are large and juicy. Today I grow my own raspberries and also pick wild raspberries to fulfill all the raspberry recipes. Twenty years ago, I picked seventy-five quarts of wild raspberries. Walking back through overgrown fields and getting caught in the thorny wild roses in the wilds would not deter me. The call of the berries was there.

PHOTO ~ *Mary Jane Brucker Perry,* my mother

Rosemary's Pie Pastry

. . . . . .

Lard is the unheard-of ingredient today to make pastry for pies. Many years ago, lard, instead of shortening, was used to make the flakiest of piecrusts. We kept lard in a five-gallon covered bucket in the basement. Not only was lard used for pies, but also to fry meat, chicken and pancakes, and to pop popcorn. My mother remembers taking lard sandwiches to school for lunch during the depression years.

I found this piecrust recipe in the sixties when I was first married, and it has been a real good one. It tastes almost like a cookie, light and flaky. Baking powder is a surprise ingredient. At home we would put the pie pastry trimmings from a pie in a flat pan, poke holes in each trimming with a fork and sprinkle with cinnamon-sugar. Bake trimmings in a 400° oven for about 8 to 10 minutes. I still make cinnamon crusts from the trimmings.

3 cups all-purpose flour
1 tablespoon sugar
3/4 teaspoon salt
1/2 teaspoon baking powder
1 1/4 cups shortening
1 egg, beaten
5 tablespoons water
1 tablespoon cider vinegar

In a large bowl mix together the flour, sugar, salt and baking powder.
Cut in the shortening until mixture resembles small peas.
In a small bowl combine the egg, water and vinegar. Sprinkle 1/2 of the egg mixture over flour
    mixture and mix lightly with a fork. Add more of the egg mixture and continue mixing until
    pastry just holds together. Gather dough together with hands and press into a ball.
Chill 15 minutes
Makes enough pastry for two 2-crust pies, depending on thickness of pastry desired.

Note: Pastry can be divided into 4 round discs, put into freezer bags, and frozen.
    Use as needed. Will defrost at room temperature in 1 hour.

Never-Fail Pie Meringue

. . . . . .

1 tablespoon cornstarch
6 tablespoons sugar
1/2 cup water
Pinch of salt
3 egg whites, at room temperature
1 teaspoon vanilla

In a medium saucepan mix together cornstarch, sugar, water and salt and cook until thick and clear. Cool.

In a medium bowl, using an electric mixer on medium speed, beat egg whites until frothy. Continue beating while slowly pouring cooked mixture over, and continue beating for five minutes. Beat in vanilla.

Makes enough for an 8- or 9-inch pie.

Lemon Meringue Pie

. . . . . .

1 9-inch unbaked pastry shell, with fluted edge and pricked with a fork
1 egg white, beaten with a fork

Bake pastry shell in a 425° oven for 8 to 10 minutes, or until shell is lightly brown.
Remove pastry shell from oven and immediately coat bottom and sides with beaten egg white using
  a pastry brush. This helps to keep pastry from becoming soggy. Cool.

Filling:
1 1/4 cups sugar
1/4 cup cornstarch
3 tablespoons all-purpose flour
1/4 teaspoon salt
1 1/2 cups cold water
4 large egg yolks, slightly beaten
1/2 cup fresh lemon juice
2 tablespoons butter
1 1/2 tablespoons lemon peel, grated
Never-Fail Pie Meringue (see recipe, page 161)

Mix sugar, cornstarch, flour and salt together in a heavy medium saucepan. Gradually whisk in water.
  Bring to boil over medium-high heat and boil 1 minute, stirring constantly.
In a medium bowl whisk yolks to blend. Gradually whisk in some of the hot cornstarch mixture.
  Return mixture to saucepan and boil until very thick, stirring constantly for about 5 minutes.
  Remove from heat. Whisk in lemon juice, butter and lemon peel.
Cool completely. Spoon filling into crust. Chill while making Never-Fail Pie Meringue.
Cover cooled filling in pie shell with meringue, sealing edges to crust.
Bake in a 400° oven for 5 to 7 minutes until golden.
Serves 6 to 8.

Chocolate Meringue Pie

. . . . . .

1 9-inch unbaked pastry shell, with fluted edge and pricked with a fork
1 egg white, beaten with a fork

Bake pastry shell in a 425° oven for 8 to 10 minutes, or until shell is lightly brown.
Remove pastry shell from oven and immediately coat bottom and sides with beaten egg white using
  a pastry brush. This helps to keep pastry from becoming soggy. Cool.

Filling:
1 1/2 cups sugar
3 tablespoons cornstarch
1/2 teaspoon salt
1/2 cup cocoa powder
3 cups milk
3 egg yolks, slightly beaten in separate bowl
1 tablespoon butter
1 1/2 teaspoons vanilla
Never-Fail Pie Meringue (see recipe, page 161) *(optional)*
Whipped Cream (see recipe, page 165) *(optional)*

Mix sugar, cornstarch, salt and cocoa powder in a medium saucepan. Gradually stir in milk.
  Cook over medium heat, stirring constantly, until mixture thickens and boils. Boil for 1 minute.
  Remove from heat.
In a medium bowl whisk egg yolks to blend. Gradually stir at least half of the hot mixture into egg
  yolks. Return mixture to saucepan. Boil 1 minute more, stirring constantly. Remove from heat.
  Blend in butter and vanilla. Pour immediately into baked pie shell.
If using Never-Fail Pie Meringue, cover cooled filling in pie shell with meringue, sealing edges
  to crust or, cover cooled filling with Whipped Cream.
Bake in a 400° oven for 5 to 7 minutes until golden.
Serves 6 to 8.

Cherry Glacé Pie

. . . . .

First Grandma Perry, then Mom, made this special pie for Christmas dinner. Not just one pie, but two or three so we all would have at least one piece. Each was topped with fresh whipped cream. In our growing-up years, we whipped rich cream from our guernsey cow. Mom always used frozen cherries we picked, pitted and froze in the family freezer. Try to imagine how many cherries we prepared each year for our large family!

1 9-inch unbaked pastry shell, with fluted edge and pricked with a fork
1 egg white, beaten with a fork

Bake pastry shell in a 425° oven for 8 to 10 minutes, or until shell is lightly brown.
Remove pastry shell from oven and immediately coat bottom and sides with beaten egg white using a pastry brush. This helps to keep pastry from becoming soggy. Cool.

1 cup sugar
1/4 cup cornstarch
1 teaspoon almond extract
Few drops of red food coloring
2 1-pound, 4-ounce cans pitted tart cherries, drained, reserving 1/2 cup of juice
Whipped Cream (see recipe, page 163) or frozen whipped topping

Combine cherry juice, sugar and cornstarch in a medium saucepan. Cook over medium heat, stirring constantly, until thickened. Stir in almond extract and food coloring. Fold in cherries. Cool slightly; turn into cooled pie shell.
Before serving, top with fresh Whipped Cream or frozen whipped topping.
Serves 6 to 8.

Whipped Cream

. . . . . .

Mom would warn me: "Don't beat the cream too long, or you will have butter."

1 cup chilled whipping cream
1/4 cup sifted confectioner's sugar
1/2 teaspoon vanilla flavoring

Chill a deep bowl and beaters from an electric mixer. Place whipping cream, confectioner's sugar and vanilla flavoring in the bowl and beat together until soft peaks form. Keep refrigerated.
Makes about 2 cups.

Raspberry Glace' Pie

. . . . . .

1 9-inch unbaked pastry shell, with fluted edge and pricked with a fork
1 egg white, beaten with a fork

Bake pastry shell in a 425° oven for 8 to 10 minutes, or until shell is slightly brown.
Remove pastry shell from oven and immediately coat bottom and sides with beaten egg white using a pastry brush. This helps to keep pastry from becoming soggy. Cool.

1/3 cup sugar
1 tablespoon cornstarch
1 cup water
1 3-ounce package raspberry gelatin
5 cups fresh raspberries
Whipped Cream (see recipe, above) *(optional)*

In a medium saucepan combine sugar and cornstarch. Add the water and bring to a boil, stirring constantly. Cook and stir for 2 minutes. Remove from the heat. Stir in gelatin until dissolved. Cool for 15 minutes.
Place raspberries in the cooled crust. Slowly pour gelatin mixture over berries. Chill until set, about 3 hours.
Top with Whipped Cream, if desired.
Serves 6 to 8.

Sugar Cream Pie

. . . . . .

This family heritage recipe came from my mother. What a hit it has been for 40 years! The secret of this pie's constant success is that the filling is cooked before putting in the pie shell. This thickens and stabilizes the filling and keeps the cornstarch from combining with the crust. Butter is a must for the best flavor.

1 9-inch unbaked pastry shell, with fluted edge and pricked with a fork
1 cup white sugar
1/4 cup cornstarch
2 cups milk
1 stick butter
1 teaspoon vanilla
Cinnamon *(optional)*
Nutmeg *(optional)*

Bake pastry shell in a 425° oven until lightly brown, about 6 to 8 minutes. Remove from oven and set aside. Reduce heat to 375°.

In a medium saucepan combine the sugar, cornstarch and milk. Cook over medium heat until thick. Remove from heat and add the butter and vanilla. Stir until butter is melted.

Pour into the pastry shell. Sprinkle with cinnamon and nutmeg, if desired.

Bake in a 375° oven for 15 to 20 minutes. Let cool for 2 to 3 hours before serving.

Serves 6 to 8.

Raspberry Pie

. . . . . .

I have heard raspberries are God's fruit. I believe it! Countless raspberry pies have been made in my kitchen. The favorite pie among my children and friends is red raspberry. In late June and early July not only am I picking raspberries, but also making numerous pies. I keep a plentiful supply of pastry dough in my freezer for this special season.

1 cup sugar
Dash of salt
1 1/2 tablespoons quick-cooking tapioca
1 1/2 tablespoons cornstarch
5 cups raspberries
1 1/2 tablespoons fresh lemon juice
1 9-inch unbaked pastry shell in pie plate, and 1 pastry to top pie
1 tablespoon butter
Sugar

In a medium bowl combine the 1 cup sugar, salt, tapioca and cornstarch. Mix in the raspberries and lemon juice. Let stand 10 to 15 minutes. Pour into pastry-lined pie plate. Cut butter into 4 pieces, and place on top of pie filling.

Cover filling with the pastry top, fluting edges of pastry together. Sprinkle top of pastry with additional sugar. Cover edges of pastry with foil to prevent overbrowning.

Bake in a 425° oven for 15 minutes.

Reduce heat to 350° and bake for 45 to 50 minutes longer.

Serves 6 to 8.

Fresh Peach Pie

. . . . . .

During fresh peach season, usually in late July and August, we Perrys cannot make enough peach pies. Many are eaten and many are given away. I like to share this special treat with family and friends.

To have fresh-tasting peach pie through the winter, line a pie pan with aluminum foil, leaving enough foil on all sides to cover filling. Pour the following peach pie filling into the foil and put in freezer, uncovered, until frozen. Then cover the peaches by overlapping the foil, and label pan. When ready to use, unwrap the filling and place in a pastry-lined pie pan. Cover with top pastry and sprinkle with sugar.

Bake in a preheated 425° oven for 20 minutes. Reduce heat to 350° and bake for 50 minutes more.

3/4 cup sugar
Dash of salt
1 1/2 tablespoons quick-cooking tapioca
1 1/2 tablespoons cornstarch
1 to 2 dashes nutmeg (to taste)
1/2 teaspoon ascorbic acid (I use Fruit Fresh)
5 cups fresh, ripe peaches, sliced
1 teaspoon fresh lemon juice
1 9-inch unbaked pastry shell in pie plate, and 1 pastry to top pie
1 tablespoon butter
Sugar

In a medium bowl combine the 3/4 cup sugar, salt, tapioca, cornstarch, nutmeg and ascorbic acid.
    Mix in the sliced peaches and lemon juice. Let stand 10 to 15 minutes.
Pour peach mixture into a pastry-lined pie plate. Cut butter into 4 pieces and place on top of filling.
Cover with the pastry top, fluting edges of pastry together. Sprinkle top of pastry with additional
    sugar. Cover pastry edges with foil to prevent overbrowning.
Bake in a 425° oven for 15 minutes.
Reduce heat to 350° and bake for 50 to 60 minutes more.
Serves 6 to 8.

Apricot Pie

. . . . . .

1 1/4 cups sugar
Dash of salt
1 1/2 tablespoons quick-cooking tapioca
1 1/2 tablespoons cornstarch
1/8 teaspoon nutmeg (to taste)
1/2 teaspoon ascorbic acid (I use Fruit Fresh)
5 cups fresh, ripe apricots, sliced
1 teaspoon fresh lemon juice
1 9-inch unbaked pastry shell in pie plate, and 1 pastry to top pie
1 tablespoon butter
Sugar

In a medium bowl combine the 1 1/4 cups sugar, salt, tapioca, cornstarch, nutmeg and ascorbic acid. Add the sliced apricots and lemon juice. Let stand for 10 to 15 minutes.

Pour apricot mixture into pastry shell. Cut butter into 4 pieces and place on top of filling. Cover with the pastry top, fluting edges of pastry together. Sprinkle top of pastry with additional sugar. Cover pastry edges with foil to prevent overbrowning.

Bake in a 425° oven for 15 minutes.

Reduce heat to 350° and bake for 50 to 60 minutes more.

Serves 6 to 8.

Strawberry Pie

. . . . . .

1 9-inch unbaked pastry shell in pie plate, and 1 pastry to top pie
1 cup sugar
2 tablespoons quick-cooking tapioca
1 1/2 tablespoons cornstarch
Dash of salt
4 cups fresh strawberries
1 teaspoon fresh lemon juice
1 tablespoon butter
Sugar

In a medium bowl combine the 1 cup sugar, tapioca, cornstarch and salt. Mix in the strawberries
and lemon juice. Let stand for 10 to 15 minutes.
Pour strawberry mixture into pastry shell. Cut butter into 4 pieces and place on top of filling.
Cover with the pastry top, fluting edges of pastry together. Sprinkle top of pastry with additional
sugar. Cover pastry edges with foil to prevent overbrowning.
Bake in a 425° oven for 15 minutes.
Reduce heat to 350° and bake for 45 to 50 minutes more.
Serves 6 to 8.

Blackberry Pie

. . . . . .

*Big purple/black pies and cobblers made with blackberries are too good to describe. While baking, the aroma
of the blackberries permeates the air you breathe. Serve with a scoop of ice cream.*

1 cup sugar
Dash of salt
1 1/2 tablespoons quick-cooking tapioca
1 1/2 tablespoons cornstarch
5 cups blackberries
1 1/2 tablespoons fresh lemon juice
1 9-inch unbaked pastry shell in pie plate, and 1 pastry to top pie
1 tablespoon butter
Sugar

(continued on next page)

In a medium bowl combine the I cup sugar, salt, tapioca and cornstarch. Mix in the blackberries and lemon juice. Let stand 10 to 15 minutes.

Pour blackberry mixture into pastry-lined pie plate. Cut butter into 4 pieces and place on top of pie filling.

Cover with the pastry top, fluting edges of pastry together. Sprinkle top of pastry with additional sugar. Cover edges of pastry with foil to prevent overbrowning.

Bake in a 425° oven for 15 minutes.

Reduce to heat 350° and bake for 45 to 50 minutes more.

Serves 6 to 8.

Cherry Pie

. . . . . .

I 1/2 cups sugar
I 1/2 tablespoons quick-cooking tapioca
I 1/2 tablespoons cornstarch
Dash of salt
4 cups fresh or frozen cherries, stemmed and pitted
1/4 teaspoon red food coloring
1/8 to 1/4 teaspoon almond flavoring
I 9-inch unbaked pastry shell in pie plate, and I pastry to top pie
I tablespoon butter
Sugar

In a medium bowl combine the I 1/2 cups sugar, tapioca, cornstarch and salt. Mix in the cherries, red food coloring and almond flavoring. Let stand 10 to 15 minutes.

Pour into a pastry-lined pie plate. Cut butter into 4 pieces and place on top of pie filling.

Cover with the pastry top, fluting edges of pastry together. Sprinkle top of pastry with additional sugar. Cover edges of pastry with foil to prevent overbrowning.

Bake in a 425° oven for 15 minutes.

Reduce heat to 350° and bake for 30 to 45 minutes more.

Cool before serving.

Serves 6 to 8.

Open-faced Rhubarb Pie

. . . . .

The first fresh fruit pie of the season.

4 cups fresh rhubarb, cleaned and chopped
1 9-inch unbaked pastry shell with fluted edge
1/2 cup butter, melted
1 1/2 cups sugar
4 tablespoons all-purpose flour
1 egg, beaten

Place chopped rhubarb in the pastry shell.
In a medium bowl mix remaining ingredients and pour on top of rhubarb.
Cover pastry edges with foil to prevent overbrowning.
Bake in a 375° oven 50 to 60 minutes.
Serves 6 to 8.

Pumpkin Pie

. . . . .

2 eggs, slightly beaten
1 can (16 ounces) solid pack pumpkin
3/4 cup sugar
1/2 teaspoon salt
1/2 teaspoon cinnamon
1/4 teaspoon ginger
1/8 teaspoon cloves
1 12- to 13-ounce can evaporated milk
1 9-inch unbaked pastry shell with fluted edge
Whipped Cream (see recipe, page 165)

In a large bowl combine filling ingredients in order. Pour into pastry shell.
Bake in a 425° oven for 15 minutes.
Reduce heat to 350° and bake for 45 minutes more.
Cool. Serve with Whipped Cream.
Serves 6 to 8.

Crème De Menthe Pie

. . . . . .

Christmas is a great time to serve this pie!

Crust:
18 cream filled chocolate sandwich cookies (Oreos), crushed
5 tablespoons butter, melted

In a medium bowl mix cookie crumbs and butter together with a fork. Press into a 9-inch pie pan.

Filling:
24 large marshmallows
2/3 cup milk
2 to 3 tablespoons crème de menthe liqueur
2 tablespoons clear cocoa de menthe liqueur
1 8-ounce container frozen whipped topping

In a large heavy saucepan cook marshmallows and milk over medium-low heat, stirring constantly, until marshmallows are melted. Let cool. Add crème de menthe liqueur and clear cocoa de menthe liqueur. Cool.
Fold whipped topping into cooled marshmallow mixture. Pour into cookie-lined pie shell. Refrigerate for 1 to 2 hours.

Topping:
1 cup whipping cream
1/3 cup sugar
1 tablespoon crème de menthe liqueur

In a medium bowl whip together the cream with the sugar. Add crème de menthe liqueur and mix just until blended.
Spread on top of refrigerated pie. Refrigerate 1 to 2 hours.
Serves 6 to 8.

Cookies & Desserts

Hedgerows grew out, gnarled and tall, providing wonderful areas underneath the low-lying branches for hideouts and play areas. In the hideouts we would put our treasures. In one particular area I had a graveyard for deceased birds found on the farm, complete with rocks for headstones. In the fall the hedge produced hedge apples. The inedible apples were medium green, the size of a softball, with a seedy looking exterior. Today hedge apples are sought for fall decorating.

On and near our farm we had a butternut tree we called "Orttie" and an oak tree we called "Crickie." We often played under these trees and talked to them as friends. We gathered the butternuts in the fall along with hickory nuts and black walnuts. At one time Mick found a wild hazelnut bush. After gathering the nuts, the outer hull had to be removed; then the nut had to dry for a month or two before cracking. The hulls of the black walnuts were messy, leaving our hands and clothes stained a dark brown. The removal of the stain was time and wear. A winter pastime of my brothers, Jim and Mick, was to shell the nuts, using a stick of wood and a hammer. The nut was placed on the wood, held with their fingers, and hit with the hammer. Especially at Christmas, these luscious nuts were mixed in candies, cookies, cakes and pies.

Other popular areas to play were the ditches and the small woods at the back of the farm. There is a difference between a creek and a ditch: A creek is a natural waterway, and a ditch is dug for drainage for the farm fields. To get to these areas, we walked down two long lanes between the fields with fences lining both sides. The lanes were used to travel from field to field by Dad's tractors, wagons and farm equipment. We walked on two parallel dirt paths in the lanes made from the wheels of Dad's tractors and wagons. Watching the birds and wildlife while walking the paths of the farm lanes is embedded in my memory for life. Along the lanes were numerous wildflowers of many colors proudly picked for our Mom. In the fields we would look for arrowheads and the oval, smooth rocks used for tomahawks by Native Americans. In the winter we had fun skating and sledding on the ice-covered ditches.

PHOTO ~ *Jim and Lawrence Jr.*, my brothers

Grandma's Molasses Cookies

. . . . . .

Grandma Lydia Brucker, on my mother's side of the family, passed down this favorite. It's amazing how one recipe can survive the generations. Kathy, my younger sister, won a prize at the 4-H Fair in Pulaski County with this older generation cookie.

2 cups sugar
1 cup shortening
2 eggs, well beaten
1/2 cup dark molasses
4 cups sifted all-purpose flour
4 teaspoons baking soda
1 teaspoon salt
1 teaspoon cinnamon
1/4 teaspoon ginger
Sugar

In a large bowl beat together the 2 cups sugar and shortening until creamy. Beat in eggs and molasses.
In another large bowl mix together flour, baking soda, salt, cinnamon and ginger; add to molasses mixture. Cover and refrigerate until chilled, at least 1 hour.
Shape rounded teaspoonfuls of dough into balls. Roll in the additional sugar and place on a lightly buttered cookie sheet, 2 inches apart.
Bake in a 375° oven for 10 to 12 minutes. Remove from sheet immediately onto a wire rack or brown paper.
Makes 6 to 8 dozen.

Blonde Brownies

. . . . . .

The recipe card for these brownies is well worn after forty years of use. They don't last long!

2 2/3 cups all-purpose flour
2 1/2 teaspoons baking powder
1/2 teaspoon salt
2/3 cup (10 2/3 tablespoons) butter
2 1/4 cups brown sugar, firmly packed
3 eggs
1 to 1 1/2 cups nuts, coarsely chopped (I use walnuts)
1 to 1 1/2 cups chocolate chips

(continued on next page)

In a medium bowl mix together flour, baking powder and salt. Set aside.

In a medium saucepan, over medium-low heat, melt the butter. Remove from heat and add the brown sugar, stirring well. Cool for 10 minutes.

Pour the brown sugar mixture into a large bowl. Beat in the 3 eggs, one at a time. Add flour mixture. Stir in nuts.

Spread mixture into a buttered 13x9-inch baking pan. Sprinkle the chocolate chips evenly over the top.

Bake in a 350° oven for 25 to 30 minutes. Cool, then cut into squares.

Freezes well.

Makes 24 bars.

Cheesecake Bars

. . . . . .

The only time I use a cake mix is when I make these cookie bars. They have a "cheesecake" flavor.

1/2 cup butter
1 egg, slightly beaten
1 box yellow cake mix
1 cup pecans, chopped
2 cups confectioner's sugar
1 8-ounce package cream cheese
2 eggs, beaten
1 teaspoon vanilla
Confectioner's sugar

In a medium bowl, with hands or a pastry blender, cut the butter and egg into the cake mix, until particles are the size of peas. Spread into a buttered 13x9-inch pan. Do not press down dough. Sprinkle nuts over the top.

In a medium saucepan mix together the 2 cups confectioner's sugar, cream cheese, eggs and vanilla, cooking until melted. Pour on top of cake mixture.

Bake in a 350° oven for 35 to 45 minutes.

When cool, sprinkle confectioner's sugar on top, and cut into squares.

Makes 24 bars.

Chocolate Crackles

. . . . .

I can remember making these delicious cookies when I was young, and I'm still making them. They are a favorite.

4 1-ounce squares unsweetened chocolate, melted and cooled
1/2 cup vegetable oil
2 cups granulated sugar
4 eggs
2 teaspoons vanilla
2 cups all-purpose flour
2 teaspoons baking powder
1/2 teaspoon salt
1/2 cup walnuts, chopped
Approximately 1/2 cup confectioner's sugar

In a large bowl beat chocolate, oil and the 2 cups granulated sugar until creamy. Beat in eggs, one at a time. Add vanilla.

In a medium bowl combine flour, baking powder and salt; beat into chocolate mixture. Stir in walnuts. Chill.

By the teaspoonful, roll dough into balls. Roll to coat in the confectioner's sugar. Place on a buttered cookie sheet.

Bake in a 350° oven for 10 to 12 minutes. Cool on waxed paper or brown paper.

Makes 4 dozen.

Cocoa Drop Cookies

. . . . . .

Mom and I made these moist, soft cookies numerous times. With four brothers and three sisters (especially the brothers), they didn't stay long on the brown paper where they were placed to cool. We always cut open and flattened brown paper grocery bags to cool the cookies on when we removed them from the hot cookie sheets. To this day, I still use brown grocery bags to cool cookies.

1/2 cup shortening
1 cup sugar
1 egg
3/4 cup buttermilk
1 teaspoon vanilla
1 3/4 cups all-purpose flour
1/2 teaspoon baking soda
1/2 teaspoon salt
1/2 cup cocoa
1 cup pecans, chopped, and/or raisins

In a large bowl, using an electric mixer at medium speed, cream together the shortening and sugar until light and fluffy. Beat in egg. Stir in buttermilk and vanilla.

In a medium bowl stir together the flour, soda, salt and cocoa. Add to buttermilk mixture. Stir in nuts and/or raisins.

Chill at least 1 hour. Drop by teaspoonfuls onto a lightly buttered baking sheet.

Bake in a 400° oven for 8 to 10 minutes.

Very good with icing also.

Makes 3 to 4 dozen.

Oatmeal-Chocolate Chip Cookies

. . . . . .

Mike and Lesly, my two children, grew up with these cookies. Now their children enjoy them at their Grammy's house. Right out of the oven is the best time to eat them.

1/2 cup butter, softened
1/2 cup shortening
1 cup granulated sugar
1 cup brown sugar, firmly packed
2 eggs
1 1/2 cups all-purpose flour
1 teaspoon baking soda
1 teaspoon salt
1 teaspoon vanilla
3 cups quick-cooking oatmeal
1 to 1 1/2 cups walnuts or pecans, coarsely chopped
2 cups chocolate chips

In a large bowl beat together the butter, shortening, granulated sugar and brown sugar until light and fluffy. Add eggs, one at a time, mixing well after each.

In a medium bowl stir together flour, baking soda and salt. Add to butter-sugar mixture until blended. Add vanilla. Stir in oatmeal, nuts and chocolate chips.

Drop walnut-size spoonfuls onto ungreased baking sheets.

Bake in a 350° oven for 10 minutes. Remove from baking sheets immediately onto wire racks or brown paper.

Makes 6 dozen.

French Crème De Menthe Brownies

. . . . . .

You can't have winter holidays without these yummy treats! Allison, my godchild, requests these brownies for her special celebrations. These brownies get moister if you leave them in the refrigerator a day or two—if you are able to keep them that long!

1 cup granulated sugar
1/2 cup butter, softened
4 eggs
1 teaspoon vanilla extract
1 16-ounce can chocolate-flavored syrup
1 cup all-purpose flour
1/2 teaspoon baking powder

In a large bowl cream together the granulated sugar and butter. Blend in eggs, vanilla, syrup, flour and baking powder. Pour into a buttered 15x11x1-inch pan.
Bake in a 350° oven for 20 minutes. Brownies will fall when removed from oven.
Cool and chill in refrigerator.

Filling:
2 cups confectioner's sugar
1/2 cup butter, softened
2 to 3 tablespoons crème de menthe liqueur, or 2 to 3 tablespoons milk plus 1 teaspoon peppermint extract and 2 to 3 drops green food coloring

In a medium bowl cream together confectioner's sugar and butter. Blend in crème de menthe liqueur. Spread on chilled brownies.
Chill until firm.

Frosting:
1/2 cup butter
1 6-ounce package semisweet chocolate chips

In a small saucepan melt butter and chocolate chips over low heat, stirring constantly. Carefully spread over chilled crème de menthe filling.
Chill slightly, 1/2 hour, and cut into squares. Refrigerate. Freezes very well—just remove as many as you wish to serve.
Makes 48 bars.

Brownies with Marshmallows

. . . . . .

Moist brownies!

1 cup all-purpose flour
1/2 cup cocoa powder
1 cup butter, softened
2 cups sugar
4 eggs
2 teaspoons vanilla
1 cup walnuts, chopped
3/4 cup chocolate chips
2 cups miniature marshmallows

In a small bowl mix together the flour and cocoa powder; set aside.
In a large bowl beat butter and sugar together well. Add the eggs, one at a time, beating well
   after each. Add vanilla. Mix in cocoa mixture and the walnuts.
Spread into a 13x9-inch buttered pan. Sprinkle chocolate chips and marshmallows on top.
Bake in a 325° oven for 40 to 45 minutes.
Makes 24 bars.

Raspberry Swirls

. . . . . .

1 cup butter, softened
2 cups sugar
2 eggs
1 teaspoon vanilla extract
1/2 teaspoon fresh lemon juice
3 3/4 cups all-purpose flour
2 teaspoons baking powder
1 teaspoon salt
1 12-ounce jar seedless raspberry jam
1 cup coconut, flaked
1/2 cup pecans, chopped

(continued on next page)

In a large bowl cream together butter and sugar. Add the eggs, vanilla extract and lemon juice. Mix well.

In a medium bowl combine flour, baking powder and salt. Add to creamed mixture and mix well. Cover and chill for at least 2 hours.

Divide dough in half. On a lightly floured surface, roll each dough half into a 12x9-inch rectangle.

In a medium bowl combine jam, coconut and pecans; spread over rectangles. Carefully roll up each rectangle, starting with a long end, into a tight jellyroll. Wrap rolls in plastic wrap. Refrigerate overnight or freeze for 2 to 3 hours.

Cut rolls into 1/2-inch slices and place on buttered baking sheets.

Bake in a 375° oven for 10 to 12 minutes.

Cool on waxed paper or brown paper.

Makes 6 to 8 dozen.

Oatmeal-Raisin Cookies

. . . . . .

A timeless cookie.

2 cups butter, softened
4 eggs
2 cups brown sugar, firmly packed
2 cups granulated sugar
2 teaspoons vanilla
4 cups flour
2 teaspoons baking soda
2 teaspoons baking powder
2 cups old-fashioned rolled oats
2 cups raisins

In a large bowl mix together butter, eggs, sugars and vanilla.

In another large bowl sift together flour, baking soda and baking powder. Add to egg mixture. Add oats and raisins.

Drop by rounded tablespoonfuls onto an ungreased cookie sheet.

Bake in a 350° oven for 12 to 15 minutes.

Cool on waxed paper or brown paper.

Makes 6 to 8 dozen.

Grandma Perry's Refrigerator Oatmeal Cookies

. . . . . .

1 cup butter, softened
1 cup brown sugar, firmly packed
1 cup granulated sugar
2 eggs
1/4 teaspoon salt
1 teaspoon vanilla
2 1/2 cups old-fashioned rolled oats
1/2 cup nuts, chopped
1 1/2 cups all-purpose flour
1/4 teaspoon nutmeg
1/2 teaspoon baking soda
1 teaspoon baking powder

In a large bowl cream together butter and sugars. Add eggs and beat well. Add remaining ingredients.
   Mix well.
Chill dough overnight.
Roll dough into walnut-size balls. Place on ungreased cookie sheets and flatten.
Bake in a 375° oven for 10 to 12 minutes.
Cool on waxed paper or brown paper.
Makes about 5 dozen.

Sour Cream Cookies

. . . . .

A long-time favorite family cookie. Like a sugar cookie, with a cake-like texture.

1 cup sugar
1/3 cup butter, softened
1/3 cup shortening
2 eggs
1 cup sour cream
2 teaspoons vanilla
1/2 teaspoon salt
1 scant teaspoon baking soda
1 heaping teaspoon baking powder
3 cups all-purpose flour
1/4 teaspoon nutmeg *(optional)*

In a large bowl cream together sugar, butter and shortening. Add eggs and beat well. Add sour cream, vanilla and remaining dry ingredients.

Chill for 24 hours. Roll dough to 1/2-inch thickness on a lightly floured surface. Cut out with round or shaped cookie cutters.

(Before baking, I like to sprinkle cookies with additional sugar.)

Bake in a 350° oven for 8 minutes.

Cool on waxed paper or brown paper.

Makes 4 to 5 dozen.

Raspberry-Almond Thumbprints

. . . . . .

3/4 cup granulated sugar
1 cup butter, softened
1/2 teaspoon almond extract
2 cups all-purpose flour
1/2 cup raspberry jam or jelly (or your favorite fruit jam or jelly)

Glaze:
1 cup confectioner's sugar
1 1/2 teaspoons almond extract
2 to 3 teaspoons water

In a large bowl combine granulated sugar, butter and the 1/2 teaspoon almond extract. Beat with an electric mixer at medium speed until creamy. Reduce speed and add flour, scraping often. Continue beating until well mixed. Chill dough for 1 hour.

Shape dough into 1-inch balls. Place 2 inches apart on ungreased cookie sheets. With thumb, make indentation in center of cookie (edges may crack slightly). Fill each indentation with about 1/4 teaspoon jam.

Bake in a 350°oven for 14 to 18 minutes.

For glaze, in a small bowl stir together confectioner's sugar and almond extract. Gradually add water to make thin glaze.

Drizzle glaze over cooled cookies. Cool on waxed paper or brown paper.

Makes 3 1/2 dozen.

Rum Balls

. . . . . .

My sister, Marilyn, makes these special cookies for the holidays. They are easy to make.

1 pound vanilla cookie wafers, finely crushed
1 cup confectioner's sugar
2 tablespoons cocoa powder
1 cup nuts, finely chopped
3 tablespoons light corn syrup
1/2 cup rum
Confectioner's sugar

(continued on next page)

In a large bowl combine cookie crumbs, sugar and cocoa powder; mix well. Add nuts, syrup and rum.
   (Add more rum if dough becomes dry.)
Roll into 1-inch balls, then roll in additional confectioner's sugar.
Store in an airtight container in a cool, dry place, or refrigerate.
Makes 3 dozen.

Raspberry Cream Puffs

· · · · · ·

*Grandpa Leujay Perry always enjoyed my Raspberry Cream Puffs. We had plenty when the
red raspberries were ripe.*

1 cup water
1/2 cup butter
1 cup all-purpose flour
4 eggs
Whipped Cream (see recipe, page 165)
1/4 to 1/2 cup sweetened raspberries (can also use strawberries, peaches, or other fresh fruit,
   or pudding)
Confectioner's sugar

In a medium saucepan heat water and butter to a rolling boil. Stir in flour. Stir vigorously over low
   heat until mixture forms a ball (about 1 minute). Remove from heat. Beat in eggs thoroughly,
   1 at a time, until smooth.
Drop from a spoon onto an ungreased baking sheet into 8 rounded mounds, 3 inches apart.
Bake in a 400° oven for 45 to 50 minutes or until puffed, golden brown and dry.
Allow to cool slowly, away from drafts. Cut off tops with a sharp knife. Scoop out any soft dough.
Fill with Whipped Cream; spoon sweetened raspberries over Whipped Cream. Replace tops. Dust
   with confectioner's sugar.
Serves 8.

Baked Apples

. . . . . .

Baked apples during the winter months are always a welcome addition to any meal. Serve warm with cream, half-and-half, or a scoop of vanilla ice cream.

6 to 8 apples, washed, cored and halved (use Jonathan, Rome Beauty, Cortland or Granny Smith)
1 cup brown sugar, firmly packed, or 1 cup granulated sugar
3/4 to 1 teaspoon cinnamon
1/4 teaspoon ascorbic acid (I use Fruit Fresh) *(optional)*
2 to 3 tablespoons butter
Raisins and/or chopped nuts *(optional)*

Place apples in a buttered 9-inch square baking dish, slightly overlapping apple halves.
    Cover bottom of pan with water about 1/4 inch deep.
In a medium bowl mix together the sugar, cinnamon and ascorbic acid. Sprinkle evenly over
    apple halves.
Dot butter atop the brown sugar-cinnamon mixture.
If desired, sprinkle with raisins and/or chopped nuts.
Bake in a 375° oven for about 45 minutes, or until tender when pierced with a fork (time varies
    according to variety and size of apples).
Serves 6 to 8.

Chocolate Pudding with Coffee Sauce

. . . . . .

Another of my sister Marilyn's delicious contributions.

Cooking oil
2 tablespoons pecans or walnuts, chopped
1 cup all-purpose flour
1/3 cup granulated sugar
1/4 cup unsweetened cocoa powder, sifted
2 teaspoons baking powder
1/2 teaspoon salt
1/2 cup milk
1 egg, lightly beaten
2 tablespoons cooking oil
2 teaspoons vanilla
1 1/3 cups hot brewed coffee, or 1 1/2 tablespoons instant coffee in 1 1/3 cups boiling water
1/4 cup brown sugar, firmly packed
Confectioner's sugar or Whipped Cream (see recipe, page 165)

Coat 6 custard cups lightly with cooking oil and set on a baking sheet.
Spread nuts in a pie plate and bake in a 250° oven for 10 to 15 minutes or until fragrant.
In a large bowl stir together flour, granulated sugar, cocoa powder, baking powder and salt.
In a small bowl stir together milk, egg, the 2 tablespoons cooking oil and vanilla. Add to flour mixture; stir just until combined.
Divide batter among the custard cups.
In a small bowl mix together hot coffee and the brown sugar. Pour some of the coffee mixture over each dessert. Sprinkle with the nuts.
Bake in a 375° oven for 15 to 20 minutes or until the tops spring back when lightly touched.
Cool for 5 minutes. Sprinkle with confectioner's sugar or Whipped Cream.
Serve hot or warm.
Serves 6.

Cherry Cream Dessert

. . . . . .

Mom made this special dessert many times for our family. I would ask her to make it for my birthday. Today I make it the same, except I add toasted pecans.

Crust:
11 graham crackers, crushed
2 tablespoons granulated sugar
Pinch of cinnamon
1/2 cup butter, melted
1/2 cup toasted pecans

In a large bowl mix together the crushed graham crackers, the 2 tablespoons granulated sugar, the cinnamon and butter. Spread into the bottom of a 9-inch square baking dish.
Bake in a 350° oven for 5 minutes. Remove from oven and let cool.
Sprinkle top of crust with toasted pecans.

Filling:
1 3-ounce package cream cheese, at room temperature
1/2 cup powdered sugar
1 8-ounce container frozen whipped topping
1 21-ounce can cherry pie filling

In a large bowl mix together the cream cheese and powdered sugar. Fold in the frozen whipped topping. Spoon mixture evenly over graham cracker crust.
Let stand in the refrigerator for 1 hour.
Top with the cherry pie filling. Return to refrigerator for at least 1 hour more.
Serves 9.

Candy

A patchwork of memories glows in my mind of the many holidays our family enjoyed on the farm. Christmas on the farm seems to have its own sparkle, music and bright lights. The stars twinkle like bright lights from above; the wind provides music with crescendos rising and falling with each gust, blowing through the trees and around the farm buildings; and snow whirls through the air, piling in graceful, gentle drifts.

Many times during the weeks before Christmas, I walked Dad's farm lanes, pulling a sled behind me, back to the sand hill where he had planted pine trees. Long, clear icicles sparkling from the wire fence decorated the fencerows. I cut pine boughs with pinecones while snow showered me and sparkled in the bright sunshine. A family of cardinals flitted from bough to bough, causing quite a spectacular wonder. Bunnies hopping through the deep fluffy snow left their tracks in the white powder of winter. The sled piled high with greens, I returned to the farmhouse and my family.

Greens were used to decorate both inside and outside our home. Gathered pinecones were used to make festive wreathes to hang on walls and fill decorative bowls. Swags of pine greenery and pinecones decked doors. Mom and Dad laid pine branches on top of the flowerbed between the sidewalk and the house. The fresh smell of pine was vivid all through the Christmas season.

One of the rites of the holiday season was the trip by Dad and my brothers to the sand hill grove of pine trees. Their heads were covered with heavy hats, earflaps down over their ears and red flannel scarves around their necks. They made their annual trek down the snow-drifted farm lanes with the red International B and a two-wheeled wood trailer in tow. Each December Dad and the boys cut the tree, loaded it on the wood trailer and delivered it back to our house—a tree to decorate in our warm, cozy farm home. Meanwhile, Mom and her daughters strung popcorn and cranberry garlands in anticipation of the arrival of our tree. Mom and Dad and their eight children ceremoniously adorned our pine tree of wonder.

Christmas was a time of prolific baking of numerous candies, cookies and breads. One Christmas remembered we made eighty-seven dozen cookies. Candies made were fudges, taffy, peanut brittle, toffee, caramels and divinity. All members of the family helped with pulling the taffy. Family and friends visiting our home were served cookies and candies neatly arranged on plates and trays. Mom and I arranged cookies and candy in festively wrapped boxes and on plates. Oh! How we enjoyed giving these wrapped sweets to neighbors, friends, priests, nuns and family.

Walnut Caramels

· · · · · ·

These caramels are great with walnuts, and they are even better with hickory nuts.

1 cup butter
2 1/4 cups brown sugar, firmly packed
Dash of salt
1 cup light corn syrup
2 cups half-and-half cream
1/2 cup walnuts, chopped

Butter the sides of a heavy 5-quart Dutch oven. Melt the 1 cup butter over low heat; add brown
   sugar and salt, stirring until thoroughly combined. Stir in light corn syrup; mix well. Gradually
   add cream, stirring constantly. Cook and stir over medium heat until candy reaches firm-ball
   stage (245°), about 30 to 35 minutes. Remove from heat.
Place nuts evenly in the bottom of a buttered 9-inch baking pan. Pour syrup over nuts. Cool.
Cut caramels into small squares.
Makes about 2 pounds.

Sugared Peanuts

· · · · · ·

This is Mom Perry's recipe.

1 cup sugar
1/2 cup water
1/4 teaspoon maple flavoring
1 1/2 cups raw peanuts, shelled

Combine all ingredients in a medium saucepan.
Cook over medium heat, stirring frequently, for 10 to 15 minutes or until peanuts are coated
   with syrup. Spread peanuts on a well-buttered baking sheet.
Bake in a 300° oven for 15 minutes. Remove from oven and stir well. Return to oven and bake
   15 minutes more. Let cool.
Makes about 3 cups.

Party Mints

. . . . . .

3 cups confectioner's sugar
1 3-ounce package cream cheese, softened
Flavoring of choice (peppermint, spearmint, etc.)
Food coloring of choice
Granulated sugar

In a large bowl mix together all ingredients and roll into balls according to the size of the
  candy mold.
Dip half of each ball into granulated sugar; press sugared side into candy mold. Tap out of mold
  immediately. Place on waxed paper until dry.
Store in a tightly covered container with waxed paper between layers.
Makes 3 to 4 dozen.

Buckeye Candies

. . . . . .

*Buckeyes look like chestnuts. These candies look like buckeyes, and cast a spell on those
who eat them. "You just cannot stop with one," says my nephew, Dee.*

4 1/2 cups confectioner's sugar
1 3/4 cups peanut butter
1/2 pound (2 sticks) butter
1 6-ounce package chocolate chips
1/3 bar Para wax, or other bar wax

In a large bowl mix together the confectioner's sugar, peanut butter and butter by hand. Knead
  mixture and form into balls the size of a buckeye (almost walnut-size).
Stick a toothpick in each ball. Put balls on a cookie sheet and cover with plastic wrap. Refrigerate
  overnight or freeze for 2 hours.
In a double boiler melt chocolate chips and the bar wax together. Holding each candy by the
  toothpick, dip half of each ball into chocolate mixture, leaving the top of candy uncoated
  to resemble a buckeye.
Makes 4 to 5 dozen.

Sour Cream Sugared Nuts

. . . . . .

Special! Special! Every year for 25 years, I have made these walnut treats. Once you try them, you will too. They make great gifts for the holidays.

1/2 cup sour cream
1 1/2 cups sugar
1 1/2 teaspoons vanilla
13 ounces walnuts

In a medium heavy saucepan mix together sour cream and sugar. Using a candy thermometer, heat
   mixture to 223°, stirring constantly. Remove from heat. Add vanilla and walnuts. Stir rapidly until
   mixture has coated and sugared.
Spread onto a tray and separate nuts. Cool thoroughly. While cooling, stir once or twice.
Store in an airtight container. Will keep for 3 to 4 months.
Makes 4 to 5 cups.

Brown Sugar Fudge

. . . . . .

*An old recipe can still win new contests! Duane, my sister Marilyn's husband, won first prize at his
company's cooking contest with this yummy fudge. As long as I can remember, we've made this favorite candy,
especially at holiday time.*

2 cups brown sugar, firmly packed
1 cup granulated sugar
1 cup half-and-half cream
1/2 cup butter
1 teaspoon vanilla
1 cup nuts, chopped

In a large heavy saucepan combine sugars, cream and butter. Slowly cook to soft-ball stage (238°),
   stirring occasionally. Remove from heat. Add vanilla.
Cool to lukewarm (110°). Beat until mixture loses its gloss. Stir in nuts. Pour into a buttered
   9-inch square shallow baking pan. When cool, cut into squares.
Makes 3 dozen.

Double-Chocolate Fudge

. . . . .

Jane wins a prize for this fudge recipe.

2 1/2 cups sugar
1 cup evaporated milk
1/4 cup butter
1/4 teaspoon salt
1 1/2 cups miniature marshmallows
3/4 cup walnuts, chopped
1 teaspoon vanilla
1 6-ounce package semisweet chocolate pieces
1 6-ounce package milk chocolate pieces

In a 2-quart heavy saucepan combine sugar, evaporated milk, butter and salt. Cook over medium heat, stirring constantly, until mixture comes to a rolling boil. Boil 6 minutes, stirring often.

Remove from heat. Add marshmallows, walnuts and vanilla; stir until well blended.

Remove 1 1/2 cups hot mixture and place in a medium bowl. Add semisweet chocolate pieces and stir until well blended and chocolate is melted. Quickly spread chocolate mixture into a buttered 8-inch square baking dish.

Add milk chocolate pieces to remaining hot mixture and stir until melted. Spread evenly over top of first layer.

Cool until firm. Cut into 1 1/4-inch squares.

Makes 3 dozen.

Miriam's Fudge

. . . . . .

A friend of mine gave me his mother's prized recipe for fudge. Use black walnuts in this fudge for an outstanding taste. The flavor of the black walnuts blended with the chocolate creates a wonderful combination. This fudge is patterned after the fudges we made before the use of marshmallow cream, even though this recipe uses it. Enjoy!

2 1/2 cups sugar
1/2 can evaporated milk
1/2 cup butter, cut up
1 12-ounce package or 2 cups semisweet chocolate chips
3 ounces marshmallow cream
1/2 teaspoon vanilla
3/4 cups black walnuts or English walnuts, coarsely chopped

In a heavy medium saucepan combine the sugar, milk and butter; bring to a boil over medium-low heat. Cook for 4 1/2 minutes more after mixture starts to boil, stirring constantly with a wooden spoon. Remove from heat and fold in chocolate chips, stirring until melted. Add marshmallow cream and vanilla, then nuts. Continue to beat with wooden spoon until thickened.

Pour into a buttered 9-inch square glass pan.

Cut into pieces when cooled. Store in an airtight container, or wrap well in plastic wrap.

Makes 3 dozen.

Caramel Corn

. . . . . .

Often in the evenings, our family would listen to the radio, read or play games for entertainment.
All eight of us kids, along with Mom and Dad, would eat a dishpan full of this caramel corn in an evening.

1 cup sugar
1/2 cup dark corn syrup
1 teaspoon cider vinegar
1/4 teaspoon salt
1 tablespoon butter
1 teaspoon vanilla
1 teaspoon baking soda
3 quarts popped corn

In a heavy 2-quart saucepan mix together the sugar, syrup, vinegar, salt and butter. Cook, stirring constantly, until mixture boils. Cook to hard-crack stage (290°). Add vanilla and baking soda, stirring well. Pour immediately over popped corn and mix well.

Store in a covered jar to retain crispness.

Makes 3 quarts.

Jam, Jelly, Etc.

Home canning of garden fruits and vegetables was a summer occupation during my childhood. Before we had a freezer, we even canned meat. Summer days were filled with canning garden vegetables, bushels of fruits and many quarts of berries. The wood bushel baskets of peaches, plums, pears and apples were a mixed blessing, for we could eat all the fresh fruits as we wanted, but we also had to help can or freeze them. Each summer between plowing, planting and cultivating the farm fields, Dad and my brothers helped Mom and me remove stems from strawberries, pit cherries (using bobby pins) and remove skins from peaches. Long summer days were spent shelling peas and lima beans, snapping green beans, husking sweet corn and cutting it from the cobs. We all sat around our big farm kitchen table, engaged in work and conversation. Since my sisters were much younger, I was the only daughter at that time old enough to help.

The numerous quarts of canned fruits, vegetables, jams, jellies, relishes and pickles were stored in a separate small room in the basement of our home, called the fruit room. No windows or heat were in this room. The fruit room was lined with wood shelves on which proudly rested the harvested meals for the coming winter. Also stored in this room were the gathered eggs and fresh bushels of potatoes. Potatoes would keep for most of the winter in this cool room. Every month or so the growth of sprouts from the eyes of the potatoes had to be removed by Dad and a couple of us children.

With the onset of winter, fresh carrots, turnips and potatoes (root produce only) were preserved in a hole dug in the ground behind the house. Burlap lined the hole. The freshly dug unwashed vegetables were laid in the hole, topped with burlap and covered with dirt. The vegetables were dug for dinner preparation. Bushels of apples were buried in the barn beneath the hay and straw to keep them from freezing. We used these methods before second refrigerators appeared in basements and garages.

PHOTO ~ *One of Dad's Barnyards*

Preparations for Making Jams and Jellies

. . . . . .

Wash jars and bands.

In a large pot, boil jars for 3 to 5 minutes. Remove as needed to fill.

Always use new flat lids. They cannot be reused.

Place flat lids in a saucepan with water to cover. Bring to a boil and remove as needed.

Cover jars with two-piece lids. Screw bands tightly.

Invert jars for 5 minutes, and then turn upright (or follow water bath method recommended by USDA).

After jars cool, check seals.

Let stand at room temperature for 24 hours.

You may then put in a cool, dry place or freeze.

Berry Juice

. . . . . .

Crush berries thoroughly, one layer at a time. Place 3 layers of damp cheesecloth or jelly bag in a large bowl. Pour prepared fruit into cheesecloth. Tie cheesecloth closed; hang and let drip for several hours or overnight.

Red, Purple or Black Raspberry Jelly

. . . . . .

1 box fruit pectin
4 cups prepared raspberry juice
1/2 teaspoon butter
5 1/2 cups sugar

Measure sugar and set aside. In a Dutch oven mix pectin into raspberry juice. Add butter. Cook over high heat and bring to a full rolling boil, stirring constantly. Immediately stir in all sugar. Bring to a full rolling boil and boil 1 minute, stirring constantly. Remove from heat. Skim off foam with a metal spoon and discard.

Ladle quickly into prepared jars, filling to within 1/8 inch of tops. Wipe jar rims and threads. Cover with two-piece lids. Screw bands tightly.

Makes about six 1-cup jars.

Blackberry Jelly

. . . . . .

3 3/4 cups prepared blackberry juice
4 1/2 cups sugar
1 box fruit pectin
1/2 teaspoon butter

Measure sugar and set aside. In a Dutch oven mix pectin into blackberry juice. Add butter. Cook over
   high heat and bring to a full rolling boil, stirring constantly. Immediately stir in all sugar. Bring to
   a full rolling boil and boil 1 minute, stirring constantly. Remove from heat. Skim off foam with a
   metal spoon and discard.
Ladle quickly into prepared jars, filling to within 1/8 inch of tops. Wipe jar rims and threads.
   Cover with two-piece lids. Screw bands tightly.
Makes about six 1-cup jars.

Elderberry Jelly

. . . . . .

*My youngest brother Mick makes this yummy jelly from elderberries he gathers from the fencerows on his
farm. He provides his three grown children with an endless supply of jellies, jams, pickles and many other
home-canned fruits and vegetables. Even after the June 1998 tornado riddled his home, barns and many
huge oak trees, he still finds time to collect wild berries to make his many fine delicacies.*

3 quarts elderberries
1/2 cup fresh lemon juice
7 cups sugar
2 pouches liquid fruit pectin

Remove stems from the berries; wash and drain. Crush berries and transfer to a large saucepan.
Bring berries to a simmer over medium-low heat; simmer for 15 minutes. Place berries in a jelly bag
   and let drip.
In a large saucepan mix together 3 cups berry juice, lemon juice and sugar; bring to a hard boil. Add
   liquid fruit pectin; boil hard for 1 minute more. Skim off foam.
Ladle quickly into prepared jars, filling to within 1/8 inch of tops. Wipe jar rims and threads. Cover
   with two-piece lids. Screw bands tightly.
Makes eight 1-cup jars.

Clover Jelly

. . . . . .

Yes! It's clover jelly. Mick makes this jelly from pink clover blossoms he gathers from his field on his present-day farm in Pulaski County. He surprised me with this one, just when I thought I had made every kind of jelly known.

1 quart clover blossoms, freshly picked
1 quart water
1 package dry fruit pectin
2 tablespoons fresh lemon juice
4 1/2 cups sugar

Rinse clover blossoms and simmer in the 1 quart of water for 3 minutes. Strain the blossoms through a fine strainer. Discard the blossoms.

Measure 3 cups strained clover liquid into a 2- to 3-quart saucepan. Add pectin; bring to a full boil. Add the lemon juice and sugar; boil for three minutes more. Skim off foam.

Ladle quickly into prepared jars, filling to within 1/8-inch of tops. Wipe jar rims and threads. Cover with two-piece lids. Screw bands tightly.

Makes five to six 1-cup jars.

Basil Jelly

. . . . . .

You can smell fresh basil from across the room. Try this jelly with your favorite beef or fish, or as an appetizer on crackers with butter or cream cheese.

1 1/2 cups firmly packed fresh basil leaves, rinsed, well drained and minced
2 1/4 cups water
3 tablespoons strained fresh lemon juice
3 1/2 cups sugar
1 drop of green food coloring
1 3-ounce pouch plus 2 tablespoons liquid pectin

In a medium saucepan combine the basil and water and bring the water to a full boil, covered, over moderately low heat.
Remove the pan from the heat and let the mixture steep, covered, for 15 minutes.
Ladle the mixture into a jelly bag set over a large heatproof bowl and let it drip, undisturbed, for 1 hour. Do not squeeze the jelly bag, but occasionally rub it gently and scrape the juices from the outside with a spatula into the bowl. If there is less than 1 3/4 cups of the basil infusion, pour a small amount of hot water into the jelly bag and let the mixture drip until there are 1 3/4 cups basil infusion.
In a heavy 4-quart saucepan combine the basil infusion, the lemon juice, the sugar and the food coloring; cook the mixture over high heat, stirring constantly, until it comes to a full rolling boil that froths up toward the top of the kettle and cannot be stirred down.
Stir in the pectin; bring the mixture to a full rolling boil, stirring constantly, for 1 minute.
Remove from the heat; skim off foam with a metal spoon and discard.
Ladle quickly into prepared jars, filling to within 1/8 inch of tops. Wipe jar rims and threads. Cover with two-piece lids. Screw bands tightly.
Makes about four 1-cup jars.

Red, Purple or Black Raspberry Jam (Seedless)

. . . . . .

This is the ultimate jam. At our annual Kiwanis Club auction, my red and purple raspberry seedless jams go for $32.00 a cup. More time is involved, but the results are worth it.

5 cups raspberry juice and pulp
7 cups sugar
1 box fruit pectin
1/2 tablespoon butter

Using a spoon, press raspberries (a few at a time depending on size of sieve) through a fine sieve. When all juice and pulp has been pressed through sieve, discard seeds.
Measure sugar and set aside.
Mix pectin into pulp in a Dutch oven. Add butter. Place over high heat and bring to a full rolling boil, stirring constantly. Immediately stir in all sugar. Bring to a full rolling boil and boil 1 minute, stirring constantly. Remove from heat and skim off foam with a metal spoon and discard.
Ladle quickly into prepared jars, filling to within 1/8 inch of tops. Wipe jar rims and threads. Cover with two-piece lids. Screw bands tightly
Makes about eight 1-cup jars.

Apple-Cinnamon Brandied Honey

. . . . . .

I have given this honey to many for a Christmas gift. Use on hot biscuits, rolls and toast; as an ice cream topping; and in hot tea as a sweetener.

6 cups honey
6 tablespoons brandy
16 to 18 (2- to 3-inch) cinnamon sticks
64 to 72 dried apple slices

Combine the honey and brandy in a large saucepan over low heat. Do not boil.
Place 2 cinnamon sticks and 6 to 8 dried apple slices in each hot, sterilized 1-cup jar.
Ladle warmed honey and brandy into jar, filling to within 1/8 inch of tops. Wipe jar rims and threads. Cover with two-piece lids. Screw bands tightly.
Makes eight to nine 1-cup jars.

Tomato-Walnut Jam

. . . . .

2 pounds firm ripe tomatoes, sliced (I use Roma tomatoes)
4 cups sugar
Juice of 2 lemons
Grated zest of 1 lemon
1/2 cup walnuts, chopped

Place the tomatoes in a large bowl and cover with the sugar. Place a dishcloth over the bowl and let stand overnight.

The next day, transfer the tomato-sugar mixture to a large, wide saucepan and bring the mixture to a boil.

Add the lemon juice and the zest. Reduce heat slightly to a slow boil and cook until the jam reaches setting point, about 30 minutes. Stir in the walnuts and cook for 2 minutes more. Remove the jam from the heat and let stand for another 10 minutes. Stir well again, and ladle the jam into warmed, sterilized jars and seal.

The jam may be eaten after 1 month.

Makes about four to six 1-cup jars.

Hot Pepper Jam

. . . . .

Serve this as an appetizer; spread assorted crackers with cream cheese spread, then top with Hot Pepper Jam.

2 cups prepared peppers (use 1 medium red pepper, 12 red chilies and 8 jalapeño peppers)
3/4 cup vinegar
3 1/2 cups sugar
1/2 teaspoon butter
1 pouch liquid fruit pectin

Halve peppers and discard seeds. Finely chop peppers or pulse in food processor, using stainless steel blade. Drain, if necessary.

Measure 2 cups into a 6- to 8-quart saucepan. Add vinegar. Mix sugar thoroughly into peppers; add butter. Cook over high heat and bring to a full rolling boil for 1 minute, stirring constantly. Immediately stir in pectin. Bring to a full rolling boil, stirring constantly. Remove from heat and skim off foam with a metal spoon and discard. Ladle quickly into prepared jars, filling to within 1/8 inch of tops. Wipe jar rims and threads. Cover with two-piece lids. Screw bands tightly.

Makes about four 1-cup jars.

Red Onion Jam

. . . . . .

This pretty gourmet jam is another hit at our annual Kiwanis auction.

3 cups (about 1 pound) red onions, peeled, quartered and thinly sliced
1 1/2 cups apple juice
1/2 cup red wine vinegar
1 1/2 teaspoons rubbed sage
1/2 teaspoon pepper
4 cups granulated sugar
3/4 cup light brown sugar, firmly packed
1 box fruit pectin
1/2 teaspoon butter

Measure 3 cups red onions into a 6- or 8-quart heavy pot. Add apple juice, vinegar, sage and pepper; mix thoroughly.
Measure sugars into a medium bowl. Stir pectin into onion mixture in pot. Add butter. Cook over high heat; bring to a full rolling boil, stirring constantly. Immediately stir in all sugar.
Bring to a full rolling boil for 1 minute, stirring constantly. Remove from heat and skim off foam with a metal spoon.
Ladle quickly into prepared jars, filling to within 1/8 inch of tops. Wipe jar rims and threads. Cover with two-piece lids. Screw bands tightly.
Makes about six 1-cup jars.

Grandmother's Peach Jam

. . . . . .

6 cups peaches, diced
6 cups sugar
1 to 2 teaspoons ascorbic acid (I use Fruit Fresh)
1/4 cup fresh lemon juice

In a Dutch oven bring peaches, sugar, ascorbic acid and lemon juice to a boil. Reduce heat and simmer for 40 to 45 minutes.
Ladle quickly into prepared jars, filling to within 1/8 inch of tops. Wipe jar rims and threads. Cover with two-piece lids. Screw bands tightly.
Makes six 1-cup jars.

Grape Jam

. . . . .

The flavor of this jam is wonderful, due to cooking the grapes in the skins.

4 cups grapes, firmly packed
3 cups sugar

In a large bowl mash grapes and sugar together with potato masher.
Place in a Dutch oven and bring to a boil. Simmer for 20 to 25 minutes.
Run cooked mixture through a colander to remove seeds. Discard seeds.
Ladle quickly into prepared jars, filling to within 1/8 inch of tops. Wipe jar rims and threads.
   Cover with two-piece lids. Screw bands tightly.
Makes four 1-cup jars.

Quince Honey

. . . . .

A friend grows quinces (a rare fruit sometimes found at old homesteads). Quinces are distantly related to apples and pears, and originally came from Turkey and Iran. They are firm with a deep yellow color, fuzzy like a peach and rather dry. Quince is intoxicating—in the aroma you notice jasmine, vanilla and pineapple. When cooked, they turn to a deep pink color. For the last three or four years, Lynn has provided the quinces and I make the quince honey; then we share the bounty. I take delight in journeying back in time.

3 cups water
3 cups pineapple juice
3 cups sugar
7 cups quinces, cored and quartered
Juice of 2 lemons
1/2 to 1 teaspoon cinnamon *(optional)*
1/2 cup brandy *(optional)*

Combine water, pineapple juice and sugar in a large, deep pot. Bring to boil and boil 5 minutes.
Add quinces and cook until fruit has a clear red color and syrup is almost at jelling point, about
   1 hour (or longer to get jelling consistency of pulp). If pulp is too thick, add additional water.
   As mixture thickens, stir frequently to prevent sticking. Remove pot from heat.
Put mixture through a colander to remove skins. Discard skins. Add the lemon juice and, if desired,
   cinnamon and brandy. Stir well; reheat to simmering.
Ladle quickly into prepared jars, filling to within 1/8 inch of tops. Wipe jar rims and threads.
   Cover with two-piece lids. Screw bands tightly.
Makes about 5 pints.

Rosemary-Quince Honey

. . . . .

Make the Quince Honey (see recipe, page 207), stirring in 2 tablespoons chopped *fresh rosemary* right before putting mixture in jars. Fill jars as directed.

Cinnamon-Quince Honey

. . . . .

Make the Quince Honey (see recipe, page 207), stirring in 1/4 to 1/2 cup *red cinnamon candies*. In a large saucepan stir over low heat to melt candies. Fill jars as directed.

Salsa

. . . . .

3 cups tomatoes, chopped
1 1/2 cups sweet peppers, seeded and chopped
1 1/2 cups hot peppers, seeded and chopped
3/4 cup onion, chopped
1 tablespoon salt
5 to 6 garlic cloves, minced
1 6-ounce can tomato paste
1 cup white vinegar (at least 5% acidity)

In a large saucepan bring all ingredients to boiling. Simmer for 1 hour, stirring often.
Ladle into hot, sterilized jars and seal.
Process salsa in hot water bath for 30 minutes.
Makes 3 to 4 pints.

Hot Dog Relish

. . . . . .

My brother Jim married Mary Gudas thirty-two years ago. This is one of her Lithuanian mother's recipes.
Use this relish for more than hot dogs. It is great on hamburgers, brats and sausage.

5 cups cucumbers, finely chopped
3 cups onions, finely chopped
2 hot peppers (red jalapeño and/or red chilies), finely chopped
2 cups celery, finely chopped
2 green bell peppers, finely chopped
3/4 cup salt

Combine vegetables and salt in a large glass, plastic or crock container. Pour 1 1/2 quarts water
over ingredients. Let stand overnight.
Drain vegetables. Transfer drained vegetables to a large 4- to 6-quart heavy pan.

Mix in:
3 cups sugar
2 teaspoons mustard seeds
1 quart white vinegar (at least 5% acidity)

Bring mixture to simmer. Simmer for 10 minutes.
Ladle into hot, sterilized pint jars. Seal.
Process relish in hot water bath for 30 minutes.
Makes 6 pints.

13-Day Sweet Pickles

. . . . . .

A cherished friend, Phyllis, shared this recipe with me.

Place 2 gallons fresh young *cucumbers,* sliced in a five-gallon crock or plastic bucket. Dissolve 1 pint of *pickling salt* in 1 gallon of boiling water; pour over cucumbers. Let stand seven days, stirring every day and skimming mold off top.

8th Day: Pour off the brine. Cover pickles with clear boiling water.
9th Day: Pour off the water. Cover pickles with clear boiling water.
10th Day: Pour off the water. Dissolve alum (size of walnut) in boiling fresh water and pour over pickles.
11th Day: Pour off alum water.

Boil together and pour over pickles:
4 quarts sugar (8 pounds)
2 1/2 quarts cider vinegar (at least 5% acidity)
2 tablespoons whole allspice
1 teaspoon crushed cinnamon bark

12th Day: Drain syrup from pickles into a large kettle. Reheat syrup and pour over pickles.
13th Day: Drain syrup from pickles. Reheat syrup to a simmer.

Place drained pickles in hot, sterilized pint jars (do not pack). Ladle hot syrup over pickles to within 1/2 inch from top of jars. Seal. Process pickles in hot water bath for 30 minutes. Makes 12 to 14 pints.

Coleslaw for Freezing

. . . . . .

My mother gave this recipe to me over thirty years ago. It's good!

1 teaspoon salt
1 medium cabbage, shredded
1 carrot, grated
1 green pepper, chopped

In a large bowl combine salt with cabbage; let stand 1 hour. Squeeze out excess moisture. Add carrot and pepper.

Dressing:
1 cup cider vinegar
1/4 cup water
1 teaspoon whole mustard seeds
2 cups sugar
1 teaspoon celery seeds

In a large saucepan combine dressing ingredients and boil 1 minute. Cool to lukewarm; pour
    over cabbage mixture.
Transfer to a freezer container; cover and freeze.
Coleslaw thaws in just a few minutes for serving. Leftover slaw can be refrozen.
Makes 2 quarts.

Herbed Tomato Vinegar

Herbed Tomato Vinegar is a favorite of mine to give as a gift.

12 dried tomato halves
10 large sprigs of fresh rosemary
1 cup fresh basil leaves
1/2 cup fresh oregano leaves
8 cloves of garlic, peeled and cut in half
1 teaspoon whole peppercorns
3 12-ounce bottles red wine vinegar

Combine first 6 ingredients in a 1-gallon, sterilized glass jar.
In a large saucepan heat vinegar to just below boiling. Pour over ingredients in jar. Cover and
   seal securely.
Let stand in a cool, dark place for 2 weeks. After 2 weeks, strain through coffee filters, and bottle.
Makes about 5 cups.

Raspberry or Blackberry Vinegar

This vinegar adds a rich, fruity flavor to salads, meat marinades, sauces and summer fruits.

12 ounces (4 to 5 cups) blackberries or raspberries, rinsed and patted dry
2 cups white wine vinegar

Place the berries in a clean 1-quart mason jar. In a small saucepan over medium heat, heat the vinegar
   until very warm (not boiling). Pour the vinegar over the berries; cover and let steep in a cool,
   dry place for 10 days.
Strain the vinegar through a funnel lined with cheesecloth or a coffee filter, pressing the pulp against
   the side of the funnel to extract all of the juice. Pour into a sterilized jar. Seal and store in a cool,
   dry place.
Makes about 1 quart.

Refreshers

Saturdays were "going-to-town" days. Not many people today say they are "going to town". Most people today live in towns, cities or suburban areas. Going to town caused much excitement, with every-one ready to go in a matter of minutes. All the groceries were bought for the week and any other errands in town were done. Saturdays also meant getting Sunday's main meal started. Usually we baked the pies, cakes, bread, rolls, etc., on Saturday.

Saturday evening was bath time. In the early toddler years, baths were given in the large laundry tubs used for doing the laundry. (These same tubs served as mini swimming pools outside in the hot summer.) There was no bathroom in the old home across the road. Mom heated the water on the stove for our baths, often bathing two children at once. Our new home in 1949 had our first bathroom, and just three bed-rooms: one for Mom and Dad, one for the boys and one for the girls. Sharing was a necessity and an advantage.

It was unheard of for any of the stores in town to be open on Sunday. For Sundays were meant to go to church, and to rest the remainder of the day or to visit with friends and family. No work was done on Sundays, except for the making of the meals. Sunday breakfasts were considered special with fresh side meat (uncured bacon) or sausage, fried potatoes, eggs, homemade sweet rolls, milk and/or hot chocolate. Dinner was a large meal served mid-afternoon. Popcorn and apples were the usual Sunday evening snack.

PHOTO ~ *My father holding me, Jim and Lawrence Jr.*

Raspberry Balm Wine

. . . . .

4 cups dry white wine
1/4 cup sugar
1 pint fresh raspberries
1/4 cup lemon balm
1/2 cup brandy

In a large non-aluminum saucepan combine the wine and the sugar and bring to a boil. Remove from heat immediately. Stir to dissolve the sugar, and cool to tepid.

Put the fresh raspberries and lemon balm in a clean, large glass jar with a tight-fitting lid. Pour the brandy and the wine mixture over them.

Steep in a cool, dark place for 2 to 3 days. (I steep in the refrigerator.)

Filter through a coffee filter.

Keep refrigerated in a glass jar with a tight-fitting lid. Will keep in refrigerator for 3 months.

Makes 5 to 6 cups.

Strawberry Balm Wine

. . . . .

At my sister Jane's shower, I served this luscious wine.

4 cups dry white wine
1/4 cup sugar
1 pint fresh strawberries
1/4 cup lemon balm
1/2 cup brandy

In a large non-aluminum pot combine the wine and the sugar and bring to a boil. Remove from heat immediately. Stir to dissolve the sugar, and cool to tepid.

Put the fresh strawberries and lemon balm in a clean, large glass jar with a tight-fitting lid. Pour the brandy and the wine mixture over them.

Steep in a cool, dark place for 2 to 3 days. (I steep in the refrigerator.)

Filter through a coffee filter.

Keep refrigerated in a glass jar with a tight-fitting lid. Will keep in refrigerator for 3 months.

Makes 5 to 6 cups.

Chamomile Wine

. . . . . .

4 cups red or white wine
1/2 cup fresh chamomile flowers
1 tablespoon orange peel
1 teaspoon lemon peel
3 tablespoons brown sugar

Place all ingredients in a glass jar with a tight-fitting lid. Steep in a cool, dark place for 1 week.
Filter through a coffee filter.
Keep refrigerated in a glass jar with a tight-fitting lid. Will keep in refrigerator for 3 months.
Makes 5 to 6 cups.

Peach Wine

. . . . . .

4 cups dry white wine
1/4 cup sugar
6 ripe peaches, pitted, peeled and sliced
1/4 cup cinnamon basil
1/2 cup brandy

In a large non-aluminum saucepan combine the wine, sugar and peaches and simmer for 10 minutes.
  Remove from heat immediately. Stir to dissolve the sugar, and cool to tepid.
Put the cinnamon basil in a clean, large glass jar with a tight-fitting lid. Pour the brandy and the
  wine mixture over the cinnamon basil.
Steep in a cool, dark place for 2 to 3 days. (I steep in the refrigerator.)
Filter through a coffee filter.
Keep refrigerated in a glass jar with a tight-fitting lid. Will keep in refrigerator for 3 months.
Makes 5 to 6 cups.

Raspberry Liqueur

. . . . . .

Delicious and different! Sip it as a light after-dinner drink. It may take the place of dessert.

4 cups fresh raspberries
3/4 cups rose geranium leaves
1/2 cup lemon verbena leaves
4 cups vodka
1/2 cup white wine
1 cup sugar
1/2 cup water

Combine the raspberries, geranium leaves, lemon verbena leaves, vodka and wine in a clean, large jar
    with a tight-fitting cover. Place in a cool, dark place to steep for 1 month.
Crush the berries slightly with a wooden spoon or potato masher and steep for another 4 days.
Strain the liquid, pressing as much juice as possible from the berries, then filter through a coffee filter.
In a small saucepan combine the sugar and water and boil until sugar is dissolved. Cool; then
    gradually stir into the liqueur.
Bottle and age for an additional 3 weeks in a cool, dark place.
Makes 8 to 10 cups.

Raspberry Framboise

. . . . . .

*Try this in white-chocolate cheesecake, over fresh fruit and over ice cream. The fragrant syrup can be sipped
over crushed ice, added to sparkling water for a cooler, to champagne for an aperitif or over chipped ice.
It is truly exceptional.*

1 1/2 quarts fresh raspberries
2 1/2 cups brandy
Approximately 1 3/4 cups sugar

Lightly crush the raspberries. Place raspberries in a clean, large glass jar (about an 8-cup jar)
    with the brandy. Close tightly and leave in a cool, dark, dry place for 2 months.
Strain the liqueur through a nonmetallic sieve lined with cheesecloth. Measure the liquid; stir in
    3/4 cup plus 2 tablespoons sugar for every 2 1/2 cups of liquid. Cover and leave for 2 days,
    stirring occasionally to dissolve the sugar.
Pour into clean bottles, seal and store in a cool, dark, dry place for at least 6 months before using.
Makes 8 cups.

Coffee-Flavored Liqueur

. . . . . .

My sister, Jane, made each of our families a bottle of this coffee-flavored liqueur one year for Christmas.

2 cups sugar
3 1/2 cups water
8 teaspoons instant coffee

Simmer for one hour, remove from heat and add:
1 liter vodka
4 teaspoons vanilla

Makes about 2 liters.

Lemon Cordial

. . . . . .

3 1/4 cups 100-proof vodka
Zest from 6 lemons
1 3/4 cups sugar
3 1/4 cups water

Pour vodka into an 8-quart glass jar and add lemon peels. Cover with plastic wrap and let stand at room temperature 1 week.

After 1 week, line a sieve with a coffee filter and place over another large bowl. Pour vodka mixture through sieve and discard lemon peels.

In a 2-quart saucepan mix sugar with water. Heat over medium heat and simmer for 2 minutes. Cool completely.

Add cooled syrup to vodka mixture. Pour cordial into bottles with tight-fitting stoppers or lids.

Cordial is best served very cold. Try serving from the freezer, very cold and syrupy.

Makes 7 cups.

PHOTO ~ *Mary Jane Brucker Perry*, my mother

Index

HERB SEASONINGS
Cajun Seasoned Salt~12
Rosemary's Fish Seasoning Mix~12
Rosemary's Pork Seasoning~11
Rosemary's Roast Beef Seasoning~10
Rosemary's Soup Seasoning Mix~11

FINGER FOODS
Black Bean Dip~22
Cocktail Shrimp~18
Crab Dip~22
Cucumber Spread~23
Fresh Tomato Chili Dip~20
Hill Country Salsa~23
Marinated Mushrooms~17
Salmon Party Spread~21
Shrimp Cheese Ball~15
Shrimp Spread~21
Shrimp-Stuffed Eggs~19
Smoked Salmon-Stuffed Cherry Tomatoes~18
Sun-dried Tomato and Pesto Torte~16
Tomato Basil Sandwiches~14
Tomato Cheese Spread~20

BREAD
Anise Bread (Bread of the Dead)~35
Black Pepper-Cheese Bread~33
Egg Bread Loaves~26
English Muffin Bread~34
Honey Wheat Bread~32
Raisin Rye Bread~28

Rosemary's Potato Rolls~27
Sourdough French Bread~38
Spiral Cinnamon-Raisin Bread~30
Sweet Potato Rolls~37
Tomato-Cheese Bread~30
Tomato Dinner Rolls~36
Walnut Bread~29
Whole-Wheat Raisin Loaf~40

BREAKFAST BREADS
Apple-Nut Bread~55
Apricot Streusel Coffee Cake~47
Baked Porridge~53
Blueberry Tea Loaf~54
Bohemian Braid~44
Buttermilk Carrot Bread~58
Caramel-Pecan Rolls~46
Cinnamon Rolls~43
Cinnamon-Sugar~48
Cinnamon Twists~50
Date, Walnut and Brazil Nut Loaves~57
Egg Pancakes~51
German Sour Cream Twists~49
Orange Glaze~45
Orange Rolls~45
Sweet Roll Dough (basic recipe)~42
Sour Cream-Blueberry-Banana Bread~56
Sour Cream Pancakes~52
Sugared Golden Puffs~48
Tea Ring~43
White Glaze~51

MUFFINS
Apple-Walnut Muffins~64
Banana-Raspberry Muffins~71
Banana-Nut Muffins~72
Bleeding Heart Muffins~67
Blueberry Muffins~61
Cheddar-Raisin Muffins~66
French Breakfast Muffins~60
Garden Herb Muffins~63
Heartland Apple Nut Muffins~68
Lemon-Poppy Seed Muffins~62
Oatmeal Muffins~69
Raspberry-Oat Muffins~70
Sun-dried Tomato Muffins~65

SOUPS
Black Bean Soup~84
Corn and Cheddar Chowder~77
Corn and Potato Chowder~78
Cream of Asparagus Soup~76
Cream of Broccoli Soup with Cheese~74
Cream of Chicken Florentine~79
Cream of Reuben Soup~80
Old-fashioned Cabbage Soup~81
Rosemary's Vegetable-Beef Soup~75
Susan's Split-Pea Soup~83
Tomato and Basil Soup~78
Wild Rice Chowder~82

SALADS
Baked German Potato Salad~91
Bibb Lettuce Salad with Raspberries~99
Cauliflower, Bacon and Onion Salad~96
Cranberry-Walnut Relish~100
Creamy Pea-Potato Salad~97
Elizabeth's Salad Dressing~102
Fresh Broccoli Salad~98
Fruited Chicken Salad~90
Layered Basil-Vegetable-Pasta Salad~92
Leaf Lettuce Salad~87
Pasta and Walnut Fruit Salad~98
Rasperry Cream Dressing~102
Raspberry Delight Salad~93
Red Raspberry Salad~89

Refrigerator Pickles~101
Rosemary's Basil Potato Salad~86
Sauerkraut Salad~94
Sherried Cherry Salad~95
Shrimp Salad~94
Slaw~90
Spinach Salad~96
Strawberry Salad~93
Sweet-Sour Dressing~103
Wilted Lettuce~88

MEAT AND POTATOES
Barbecue Meal in One~109
Barbecued Hamburger~110
Beef and Noodles~107
Beef Stroganoff~108
Brye~118
Chicken and Biscuits~116
Chicken Pot Pie~115
Escalloped Chicken~114
Glazed Ham Balls~113
Ham and Asparagus Casserole~117
Ham Loaf~112
Hamburger Stew~114
Meat Loaf~106
Pasta with Shrimp and Asparagus~123
Rigatoni with Tomato-Meat Sauce~119
Rosemary's Basil-Tomato Sauce for Pasta~120
Shrimp Kabobs~121
Stuffed and Rolled Flank Steak~111
Tangy Tuna Tetrazzini~120
Uncooked Tomato Sauce~122

VEGETABLES
Baked Cabbage~129
Baked Sweet Potatoes~130
Broccoli Casserole~131
Company Mashed Potatoes~126
Creamed Onions~130
Creamed Peas and Potatoes~128
Fresh Green Beans~127
Fried Sweet Potatoes~129
Lacy French-Fried Onions~131
Sweet and Sour Beets~132

CAKE & ICE CREAM

Banana Spice Cake~140
Banana Nut Cake~141
Carrot Cake~142
Chocolate Layer Cake~134
Cream Cheese Frosting~142
Favorite Vanilla Ice Cream~147
Hickory Nut Cake~137
Homemade Frozen Custard~147
Maraschino Cherry Cake~143
Mary Jane's Frosting~144
Old-fashioned Raspberry Ice Cream~146
Peach Ice Cream~146
Peanut Butter Broiled Icing~145
Pineapple Filling~139
Raspberry Angel Food Cake~144
Rosemary's Sunshine Cake~138
Sour Cream-Chocolate Frosting~135
Vanilla Ice Cream~145
White Whipped Frosting~135
Zucchini-Chocolate Cake~136

CHEESECAKES

Chocolate-Amaretto Cheesecake~155
Chocolate-Crème De Menthe Cheesecake~155
Coconut Cream Cheesecake~153
Creamy Chocolate Lace Cheesecake~156
Frangelico Cheesecake~151
Irish Cream Cheesecake~152
Lime Cheesecake~150
Pumpkin Cheesecake~157
White Chocolate Cheesecake~154

PIES

Apricot Pie~169
Blackberry Pie~170
Cherry Glace' Pie~164
Cherry Pie~171
Chocolate Meringue Pie~163
Crème De Menthe Pie~173
Fresh Peach Pie~168
Lemon Meringue Pie~162
Never-Fail Pie Meringue~161

Open-faced Rhubarb Pie~172
Pumpkin Pie~172
Raspberry Glace' Pie~165
Raspberry Pie~167
Rosemary's Pie Pastry~160
Strawberry Pie~170
Sugar Cream Pie~166
Whipped Cream~165

COOKIES & DESSERTS

Baked Apples~188
Blonde Brownies~176
Brownies with Marshmallows~182
Cheesecake Bars~177
Cherry Cream Dessert~190
Chocolate Crackles~178
Chocolate Pudding with Coffee Sauce~189
Cocoa Drop Cookies~179
French Crème De Menthe Brownies~181
Grandma's Molasses Cookies~176
Grandma Perry's Refrigerator Oatmeal
    Cookies~184
Oatmeal-Chocolate Chip Cookies~180
Oatmeal-Raisin Cookies~183
Raspberry-Almond Thumbprints~186
Raspberry Cream Puffs~187
Raspberry Swirls~182
Rum Balls~186
Sour Cream Cookies~185

CANDY

Brown Sugar Fudge~194
Buckeye Candies~193
Caramel Corn~197
Double-Chocolate Fudge~195
Miriam's Fudge~196
Party Mints~193
Sour Cream Sugared Nuts~194
Sugared Peanuts~192
Walnut Caramels~192

JAM, JELLY, ETC.

13-Day Sweet Pickles~210
Apple-Cinnamon Brandied Honey~204
Basil Jelly~203
Berry Juice~200
Blackberry Jelly~201
Cinnamon-Quince Honey~208
Clover Jelly~202
Coleslaw for Freezing~211
Elderberry Jelly~201
Grandmother's Peach Jam~206
Grape Jam~207
Herbed Tomato Vinegar~212
Hot Dog Relish~209
Hot Pepper Jam~205
Preparations for Making Jams and Jellies~200
Quince Honey~207
Raspberry or Blackberry Vinegar~212
Red Onion Jam~206
Red, Purple or Black Raspberry Jam (Seedless)~204
Red, Purple or Black Raspberry Jelly~200
Rosemary-Quince Honey~208
Salsa~208
Tomato-Walnut Jam~205

REFRESHERS

Chamomile Wine~215
Coffee-Flavored Liqueur~217
Lemon Cordial~217
Peach Wine~215
Raspberry Balm Wine~214
Raspberry Framboise~216
Raspberry Liqueur~216
Strawberry Balm Wine~214

Furrows and Hedgerows

You may order additional copies of *Furrows and Hedgerows* for the price of $26.25 each plus $3.00 postage and handling per book ordered. Mail below order form with payment to: *Thyme with Rosemary Books*; 2548 Robinwood Drive; Lafayette, IN 47909.

Thyme with Rosemary Books; 2548 Robinwood Drive; Lafayette, IN 47909

Please send me _____ copies of *Furrows and Hedgerows* @ $26.25 each $_____

Postage and handling . . . . $3.00 each $_____

Total enclosed . . . . $_____

(Please Print)

Make checks payable to: *Thyme with Rosemary Books*

Name _____

Address _____

Cite, State, Zip _____

Telephone _____

Thyme with Rosemary Books; 2548 Robinwood Drive; Lafayette, IN 47909

Please send me _____ copies of *Furrows and Hedgerows* @ $26.25 each $_____

Postage and handling . . . . $3.00 each $_____

Total enclosed . . . . $_____

(Please Print)

Make checks payable to: *Thyme with Rosemary Books*

Name _____

Address _____

Cite, State, Zip _____

Telephone _____